W9-CCA-459

THE JGUY'S GUIDE

The GPS for Jewish Teen Guys

Rabbi Joseph B. Meszler, Dr. Shulamit Reinharz,
Liz Suneby and Diane Heiman

JEWISH LIGHTS Publishing
Woodstock, Vermont

The JGuy's Guide:
The GPS for Jewish Teen Guys

2013 Quality Paperback Edition, First Printing

Library of Congress Cataloging-in-Publication Data
Meszler, Joseph B.
  The Jguy's guide : the GPS for Jewish teen guys / Rabbi Joseph B. Meszler, Dr. Shulamit Reinharz, Liz Suneby & Diane Heiman.
     pages cm
  Includes bibliographical references.
  ISBN 978-1-58023-721-5
  1. Teenage boys—United States—Religious life. 2. Jewish teenagers—United States—Religious life. 3. Jews—identity—United States. I. Reinharz, Shulamit. II. Suneby, Elizabeth, 1958- III. Heiman, Diane. IV. Title.
  BM727.M47 2013
  296.70835'1—dc23

                              2013031652

10 9 8 7 6 5 4 3 2 1

Manufactured in the United States of America

Cover and Interior Design: Tim Holtz

For People of All Faiths, All Backgrounds
Published by Jewish Lights Publishing
A Division of LongHill Partners, Inc.
Sunset Farm Offices, Route 4, P.O. Box 237
Woodstock, VT 05091
Tel: (802) 457-4000   Fax: (802) 457-4004
www.jewishlights.com

For Justin, Zachary, and Brooks
(JBM)

For Ryan and Zachary with love
(DBH)

For my son, Josh, with love
(EKS)

For Naomi, Yali, James, and Amalia
(STR)

B'Yachad
South Area Religious School

Presents this Book to

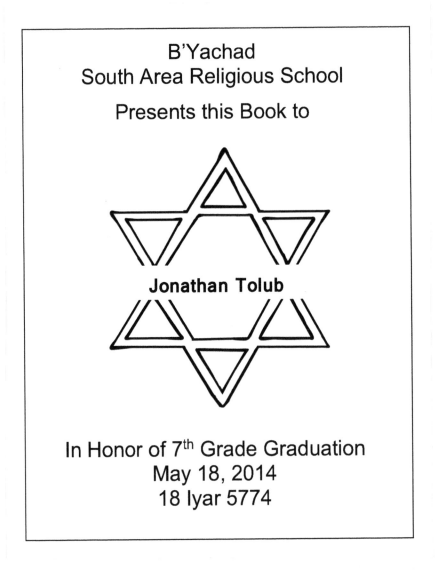

Jonathan Tolub

In Honor of 7th Grade Graduation
May 18, 2014
18 Iyar 5774

Contents

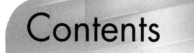

Falling in Lust, Falling in Love

Not on My Watch

Looking Inside at the Man I Want to Be

Preface

עֲשֵׂה לְךָ רַב, וּקְנֵה לְךָ חָבֵר, וֶהֱוֵי דָן אֶת כָּל הָאָדָם לְכַף זְכוּת*

Aseih l'cha rav, uk'nei l'cha chaver, vehevei dan et kol ha'adam l'chaf z'chut.

"Get yourself a teacher, find yourself a friend, and judge everyone favorably."

—*Pirkei Avot* 1:6

"Who am I? Am I cool or dorky? Do I fit in? What kind of a man will I become? And what about being Jewish—how does all that work? I've got school and my friends, sports and grades, games, homework, music, the Web, and being Jewish. Is my body really okay? I've got questions about sex. My Jewish teachers talk about God, Torah, and Israel, but I don't even know what that is really all about or what I believe. How does all this fit together?"

Life is a winding and unexpected road. When we need to know where we are and how to get where we're going, we use a GPS, a global positioning system. This book is a GPS for you, the Jewish teenage guy.

---

*We have included Hebrew phrases in each chapter. Hebrew is important because it is like Jewish glue—it helps connect and bond us. It is made of the sounds, words, and values Jews have used for centuries, still use all over the world today (especially in Israel), and will use in the future. If you know the phrase, say it out loud. If you don't, try to sound it out.

At a bar mitzvah people talk about becoming a man in the Jewish religion, but what is that supposed to mean? For sure it means you are no longer a child, but you are also not yet an adult. Fortunately, there's no one official definition of manhood, just as there is no one official way of being Jewish. That's where this book comes in.

The JGuy's Guide uses interviews from dozens of teenage Jewish guys just like you. It talks about what you are thinking about, with no judgment or criticism. It also draws on Jewish wisdom to help you figure out what becoming a man means to *you*. It interweaves how Jewish men nowadays and all the way back to biblical times answered these very questions with personal stories, surprising facts, classic texts, and provocative discussion questions.

The book is organized like the ancient Talmud—written between 200 and 500 CE—which contains opinions of hundreds of rabbis on lots of subjects, including laws, ethics, philosophy, customs, and more. There are more questions than answers. When people study the Talmud, they derive their own conclusions from the variety of opinions they've read. You can do that, too.

The JGuy's Guide borrows this approach—lots of questions and perspectives presented about an issue to help you find your own truth. And we realize you might change your mind. We promise:

✡ No preaching; no step-by-step instructions
✡ Interesting stories, ideas, and actions for you to consider
✡ To challenge stereotypes and myths
✡ Different opinions—not just from old guys, but from guys your age, too

Each chapter includes the following sections. Read the ones that appeal to you:

Personal Introduction

The confusing, ridiculous, painful, and funny questions of life that teen guys face, by Rabbi Joseph Meszler

Find Yourself a Friend

Voices of your peers, teen guys interviewed for this book

Did You Know?

Information that you may not be aware of

Get Yourself a Teacher

Lessons of "wise men"—historical and modern role models

Learn

Biblical and contemporary sources on the issue, with discussion points for groups

What Do I Think?

Space for your personal response

Text Connection

Hebrew texts containing words to remember and live by

Even though this book is written in a consistent order to make it easy to use, flip open to any page you want. We hope this book helps you see how Judaism can make your teen years a little less stressful, a little more satisfying, and a whole lot more courageous.

A Little about Us

Rabbi Joseph B. Meszler is the rabbi at Temple Sinai in Sharon, Massachusetts, where he launches at least twenty boys a year into Jewish manhood. These bar mitzvah boys tell him their stories.

Many of these boys become students at Brandeis University, where Shulamit Reinharz is a professor of sociology. Among many other books, she wrote *The JGirl's Guide: The Young Jewish Woman's Handbook for Coming of Age* (with colleague Penina Adelman and student Ali Feldman). When it was published, many said, "What about the boys?" So, Shula turned to Liz Suneby and Diane Heiman for help.

Liz Suneby and Diane Heiman are best friends. They have written fabulous books for teens and children, such as *The Mitzvah Project Book: Making Mitzvah Part of Your Bar/Bat Mitzvah ... and Your Life* and *It's a ... It's a ... It's a Mitzvah*. For Liz and Diane, writing a book for teenage boys was a natural next step.

Acknowledgments

Many thanks to Steve Gilman of Temple Sinai; Brett Lubarsky, youth programs coordinator and social media and community manager at Temple Beth Elohim in Wellesley, Massachusetts; Ira Miller, director of informal education, and Rabbi Aaron Miller, assistant rabbi, at Washington Hebrew Congregation in Washington, DC; and former Brandeis University students Mark Magidson and Adam Schwartzbaum for their valuable guidance, insight, and support, which helped us gain teen guys' perspectives.

Thank you, also, to the members of the Washington Hebrew Congregation confirmation class of 2015, teen boys of Temple

Beth Elohim, and teen boys from South Dakota, Kansas, Iowa, and Minnesota, who expressed their feelings with sincerity, care, and a good dose of humor.

We would especially like to thank those JGuys who spent a great deal of time reading and journaling: Aidan Arnold, David Blum, Sam Bunis, Joseph Duggan, Brett Fogel, Benjamin Friedman, Sam Fritz, Cyrin Gutmacher, Noah Habbe, Dean Kantor, Dennis Pilipenko, Adam Scher, Jordan Shapiro, Matthew Weiss, and Benjamin Zirps.

Finally, a big thank-you goes out to Stuart M. Matlins, publisher of Jewish Lights, and Emily Wichland, patient editor.

"When I am scared I take a deep breath and try to calm down. Then I face my fear."

"One of my biggest fears is living a pointless life. I can't imagine how disappointing it would be to look back on my life and think I should have done this or that."

Courage

I might be braver than I think.

חֲזַק וֶאֱמָץ

Chazak ve'ematz!

Be strong and courageous!
—Deuteronomy 31:7

"Probably one of my biggest fears is not being able to live up to my own expectations of myself in school. I think if I work harder in school I will definitely be able to conquer those fears."

"At camp I couldn't climb the rock wall because I was so scared. Eventually, I faced my fears, and once I got to the top it was never hard for me again."

Courage
I might be braver than I think.

Did you know that courage is a Jewish value? Courage is not the absence of fear. Courage is doing what you believe is right even though you might be afraid—of humiliation, of being excluded, of being bullied, of getting into trouble, or even of physical pain or death.

Why begin this book with a discussion about courage? Because underneath most of the challenges you face as a teen are different types of fears: fear of disappointing parents, teachers, coaches, friends; fear of being misunderstood; fear of being completely humiliated; fear of missing out or messing up. We know this, because the teen guys we've talked to told us so.

It takes courage to face fears. In fact, every part of your life—studying, taking tests, playing sports, playing music, managing friendships, engaging in romantic relationships, asking questions, speaking up—this all takes a certain amount of courage. Everyone fears different things. To become men, boys must learn to face whatever fears they have.

As North American Jewish teenagers get closer to high school graduation, many worry about where they'll go to college or to get career training. They think about whether they are going to live away from home, about what kind of people they will meet. Will they be able to afford a car? Will they find a good job? Growing up is scary and exciting at the same time.

Unfortunately, this world has too many grown men who act like immature boys. There are those who feel they always have to win, even if it means hurting people who get in their way. There are those who always have to be right and feel the need to belittle the people around them. There are others who have no idea how to apologize, show regret, or speak from the heart. Then there are those who whine, complain, and blame others rather than taking responsibility for their actions and following through on their commitments. There are bosses who want to dominate others and take all the credit for themselves. There are guys who disrespect and cheat on the people they are supposed to love and think, "What they don't know won't hurt them."

Judaism says boys become men at age thirteen, but we all know that is not really true today. It made sense hundreds of years ago when the average life span was forty years and people went to work and got married as teenagers. But today we thankfully have a longer time to grow up. As a teen, you are not yet an adult, but you are also no longer a child. You have some time to learn how to be a man.

There is still so much to learn and try. At every turn, you are going to have to ask yourself: Am I willing to keep growing by facing my fears?

Remember, you should never have to face your fears alone. Friends, older and wiser men and women, and Jewish learning are here to help you. No one is ever entirely successful on his or her own. And you have strength within you that you have not yet realized.

This book is about being ready to be a man. And that takes courage.

—RABBI JOSEPH

Find Yourself a Friend: Teen Voices

" One of my biggest fears is living a pointless
life. I can't imagine how disappointing
it would be to look back on my life and
think I should have done this or that."

"Sometimes people make decisions they
know are dangerous but choose to do
them anyway. A lot of the time it
seems foolish. I have taken risks doing
something I knew I probably shouldn't do."

" Probably one of my biggest fears is
not being able to live up to my own
expectations of myself in school. I
think if I work harder in school I will
definitely be able to conquer those fears."

"When I am scared I take a deep breath and
try to calm down. Then I face my fear."

" Everything in life is a risk, and I
take them all the time. Sometimes
I do them for no reason."

"One of my biggest fears is
living a pointless life."

" I used to be afraid of strangers. When
I was little I was scared to ride a bike
with my sister and no parent. I was

scared to be without a parent. I thought strangers were people who were always trying to hurt me. Now I relish the chance to be alone and independent."

"I have often feared things that I have overcome. This year I got alopecia, a hair loss disease. For the first month or so I couldn't handle going to school knowing I had a huge bald spot on my head. I even colored my bald spot in with a marker to match my hair. As the weeks went by, I started to realize that having a disease isn't something I can control. I finally just let it go, because all this stress wasn't needed. Now I get shots for my alopecia, and I've learned to live with it."

"At camp I couldn't climb the rock wall because I was so scared. Eventually, I faced my fears, and once I got to the top it was never hard for me again."

"I am afraid that I will do something that completely destroys my future, like being expelled from school or committing a major crime."

"One of my biggest fears is that something will happen to me because I have a disease that affects my muscles (myotonic dystrophy). My dad also has this and ended up really sick in the hospital and stopped breathing."

"My biggest fear is disappointing myself. I may disappoint myself in school, friendships, or sports. I know it will happen, but I try not to let it affect my decision making. I can't really face my fear because there is always another opportunity to disappoint. That is why it is my biggest fear, because I can't overcome it."

" My biggest fear is death. I know it's a part of life and it just happens, but I can't imagine living life without my mom, dad, sister, or grandparents or not living life at all. I think someday, a long, long time from now, I could be ready to face death, but not yet. Hopefully, life is just the beginning, and death is where it really starts to get good."

Did You Know?

⬥ *Webster's Dictionary* defines courage as "mental or moral strength to venture, persevere, and withstand danger, fear, or difficulty."[1]

⬥ President Franklin D. Roosevelt said there were four freedoms that everyone ought to have. After freedom of speech, freedom to worship, and freedom from want, President Roosevelt articulated the fourth and final freedom: freedom from fear. "There is nothing to fear but fear itself."

✡ The Holocaust was a time of great terror but also of great bravery. We cannot really imagine what it must have been like to be there at that time or what we would have done. Overwhelmingly, people arrested by the Nazis had to do whatever they were told because of fear for their families and themselves. In the Warsaw Ghetto and in the concentration camps Sobibor, Auschwitz, and Treblinka, some Jewish people took up armed resistance against their imprisoners. Others resisted by simply refusing to be dehumanized, such as washing with whatever water was available each day to show that they still thought of themselves as human beings or singing songs to children to keep them from being afraid. We can only look with awe at their courage.

✡ In Israel, teenagers graduating from high school have to be brave, as well. Hardly any graduates go directly to college after high school. Virtually all first go into the Israeli Defense Forces. They have to learn how to maintain and shoot a gun, how to run with a very heavy pack, and how to take orders and work in a team. In addition to worrying about living away from home and what kind of people they are going to meet, they also are aware that their lives will be at risk. Despite Israel being continually under scary threats, Israelis have learned to live life normally. Israeli teenagers hang out with friends, play video games, and root for their favorite soccer teams. They go to malls and eat at McDonald's. (Yes, there are kosher McDonald's restaurants in Israel.) But they also live their lives with a certain amount of courage because they have to face their fears. They do not let the threat of war or the uncertainty of their future stop them from living a joyful life. Israel has bred a courageous society.

⭐ Rabbi Nachman of Breslov said: "Know! A person walks in life on a very narrow bridge. The most important thing is not be afraid" (*Likutei Moharan* 2:48).

Get Yourself a Teacher

Major Roi Klein

The Courage to Protect His Soldiers

In 2006, Roi (pronounced "ro-ee") Klein was a major in the Israel Defense Forces, which is the Israeli army, or *Tzahal* in Hebrew, an acronym for *Tzva Haganah LeYisrael*. At the time, a terrorist group called Hezbollah had emerged in the neighboring northern country of Lebanon. At one point, Hezbollah kidnapped Israeli soldiers and shot missiles across the border into Israel without caring what they hit, destroying places where civilians live. (They even hit a residential home for the elderly.) Klein and his very famous Golani Brigade were part of the effort to invade Lebanon to stop Hezbollah. When Klein and his unit took cover in a Lebanese house, a grenade came flying in through the window. Klein said, "Report I have been killed." He then jumped onto the grenade, saying, "*Sh'ma Yisrael.*" By blocking the explosion with his body, he saved the lives of soldiers in his unit. Roi Klein has become a symbol of heroism, and two Israeli schools are named for him.

Michael Oren

The Courage to Face
His Learning Disabilities

Michael Oren has a long list of accomplishments to his credit. This American-born Israeli historian is an award-winning author and an ambassador from Israel to the United States. He graduated from Columbia University with a master's degree and from Princeton University with a master's and a PhD. Ambassador Oren has been a visiting professor at Harvard, Yale, and Georgetown Universities in the United States and at Tel Aviv and Hebrew Universities in Israel. To top that off, the *Jerusalem Post*, Israel's English-language newspaper, lists him as one of the world's ten most influential Jews. But guess what? When Michael was growing up in New Jersey, he called himself "an unsuccessful student ... fat, athletically 'uncoordinated' ... and socially inept."[2]

Here's how Oren spoke about his difficult youth when he accepted an award from the Lab School honoring outstanding achievers with learning disabilities:

> There was ... the indignity of being in what everybody in school knew was the lowest track—a special dishonor for me, coming from the Jewish community where young people were expected to excel academically.... I had always been what used to be called a "problem student." Back in my elementary school classes, I was a discipline problem and spent many hours—even days—in the principal's office.... By age thirteen, I was friendless, confidence-less, and failing out of school. I spent much of my time alone, wandering in the woods or alone in my room.[3]

It wasn't until Oren was sixteen years old that he figured out he had a learning disability called dyslexia (a learning disorder that makes it very difficult to spell or read), which affects between 5 and 10 percent of all the people in the world. Soon after, he began to get help with his dyslexia; that, in turn, helped him to earn good grades. But he still faced hurdles. For example, Oren's score of 230 (out of 800) on his college-entrance exam, called the SAT, uncovered Oren's inability to discern straight lines. When he took the SAT again with an accommodation to use a ruler, his score jumped 400 points. To this day, Oren says he must continue to muster the courage to rise above his learning disabilities.

Raoul Wallenberg

The Courage to Defy Authority

In the early 1940s, Swedish Christian diplomat Raoul Wallenberg saved tens of thousands of Jews in Budapest, Hungary, from being deported to the Nazi death camps. Wallenberg was sent to Budapest by the Swedish Foreign Ministry for the sole purpose of protecting the two hundred thousand Jews who remained in the capital. Initially he followed official procedures, issuing visas for Jews to emigrate. When that strategy was no longer sufficient to save enough Jews, he used his own ingenuity rather than traditional diplomacy. The Russian army invaded Budapest in 1945 and arrested Wallenberg because they suspected him of being a spy; Wallenberg then disappeared. It is reported that he died in the Lubyanka Prison in the KGB (Soviet national security agency) headquarters building in Moscow, Russia. Wallenberg is considered "Righteous among the Nations," an honor bestowed by the State of Israel to describe non-Jews who risked their lives during the Holocaust to save

Jews. Those who are recognized as "Righteous among the Nations" are awarded a medal in their name, a certificate of honor, and the privilege of having their name added to those on the Wall of Honor in the Garden of the Righteous at Yad Vashem, Israel's Holocaust Memorial Museum in Jerusalem.

Learn

Joshua Has Big Shoes to Fill

Moses called Joshua and said to him in front of the whole Israelite nation: "Be strong and courageous! You will go with this people into the land that the Eternal promised to their parents to give them. You shall divide it up among them. God will take the lead in front of you. God will be with you. God will not fail or abandon you. Do not be afraid or despair!"

(Deuteronomy 31:7–8)

Joshua is appointed the leader of the Jewish people when Moses steps down. Moses led the people out of Egypt, got them the Ten Commandments, and brought them through the wilderness. In other words, Joshua has some pretty big shoes to fill.

- How do you think Joshua felt when he took over?
- What are the main points of Moses's "pep talk" to Joshua?
- Have you ever prayed to God for courage? Do you know others who might have done so? What did they pray for?
- Do you think it is right to pray only when you need something?

Out of the Dark Woods

There is a legend about a young man named Israel ben Eliezer. When Israel ben Eliezer was a young boy, his father once woke him up in the middle of the night. He brought the boy, Israel, into the dark woods by the light of a lantern. When they were deep in the woods, his father blew out the light. The darkness closed in on them. "Father!" Israel cried out. "I am here, son," said his father. "But I want you to know that one day I will not be here. You might feel lost and in the dark, like now. But even then I want you to have faith in God and have courage. You are not alone."

When Israel became a young man, he took a job leading children to school. He went from house to house picking up the children, and sometimes he had to take paths through the forest. Once, the townspeople heard rumors that wild beasts roamed the forest, and the parents were afraid to let the children go. Israel convinced them, however, and the children followed him to school as usual. To keep them from being afraid, he taught them to sing a simple melody. The children sang and walked to and from school with joy. Israel ben Eliezer grew up to be one of Judaism's greatest teachers, the Baal Shem Tov (1698–1760), the founder of Hasidism.

Thinking about this Hasidic legend, consider these questions:

- ✡ What was Israel ben Eliezer's father trying to teach him by taking him into the woods?
- ✡ Why did the parents eventually let their children go to school?
- ✡ Who has taught you about courage and how?
- ✡ Have your parents ever kept you from doing something because they were afraid? Were they right or wrong?

Israel ben Eliezer taught the children to sing so they would not be afraid. What do you do when you are scared? How do you calm yourself down to face your fears?

What Do I Think?

Name something that you were once afraid of that you no longer fear, and explain why.

What are your biggest fears? Do you think someday you may no longer have them?

_____

_____

_____

_____

_____

_____

_____

_____

Can you think of times when people thought they were being courageous but they were just being foolish?

_____

_____

_____

_____

_____

_____

_____

_____

_____

_____

_____

Are there times when you took a risk for no good reason? If so, why?

_____

_____

_____

_____

_____

_____

_____

_____

_____

_____

Capture any of your additional thoughts or questions here.

_____

_____

_____

_____

_____

_____

_____

_____

_____

_____

Text Connection

Chazak ve'ematz!

Be strong and courageous!

—Deuteronomy 31:7

"You know someone is your
friend when you can talk to
him about your problems."

"Guys fight, but an hour later
we can forget about it,
and we just start hanging
out and playing sports. Girls
hang onto grudges much
longer than guys do."

Frenemies

I like my friends but not always what they do.

וַיִּכְרֹת יְהוֹנָתָן וְדָוִד בְּרִית

Vayichrot Yonatan
v'David b'rit.

Jonathan and David
sealed a pact.
—1 Samuel 18:3

"I think it is okay if friends
pull pranks or tease you
as long as you and they
are both aware that
nothing is meant by it."

"My friends at camp got
together a couple of nights
and purposefully excluded
me just to make me mad.
I was mad. I cried."

Frenemies

I like my friends but not always what they do.

Friends are tricky. They matter a lot to us. We care about what they think. We like to hang out with them. They make us laugh. With friends, we shoot hoops in a driveway, chat in the cafeteria at school, or play video games.

But friends can also be cruel. I remember sitting in school one day, and I had gotten a really bad sunburn on my neck. This kid named David snuck up behind me and slapped my neck as hard as he could. It hurt so bad I felt tears well up in my eyes, which was even more embarrassing. And I remember my so-called friends standing around and laughing as if it was the funniest thing in the world. I also knew I wanted to turn around and hit him, but he was a lot bigger than I was. Later, everyone expected me to just laugh it off and get over it.

Sometimes it seems that if you do anything different or stand out in any way it will be used against you. Anything you say or do can be cause for ridicule. People can also get you to do stupid things. Often, drinking or smoking pot goes along with some so-called friendships. You know that if you are going to a party with this person, that is what is going to happen. Maybe it is exciting, but it can also be dangerous and dumb.

Sometimes the easiest thing to do is to follow the crowd or make fun of someone else to divert attention away from you. Teenage guys often create a "culture of cruelty."[1] One thing that happened in my school is that kids would be pushed into urinals while they were peeing. If it happened to someone else, it was hysterically funny. If it happened to you, it was humiliating! Maybe you have heard or seen something like that, too.

In the eighth grade, there was a new kid at our school. Everyone called him by his last name—we'll call him Frank. It became a game to make fun of Frank because he was ... different. In some way you just couldn't put your finger on, Frank was awkward. Maybe it was his clothes. Maybe it was the way he talked. In any case, it was easy to laugh at Frank with other guys and not speak up in his defense.

One day, the gym teacher made us all sit down outside on the side of the hill next to the soccer field. He said the bullying of Frank must stop. Even while the teacher was talking, however, there were snickers and giggles. Frank, who was standing there, suddenly screamed out, "I hate it here! I wish we never came here!"

It was a heartbreaking moment. But at lunch later that day, for the first time, my friend Ryan made sure to invite Frank to sit at our lunch table. Ryan was always the kind one among us. He never said anything bad about anybody. Ryan, in his very quiet way, just went over to Frank and said, "Hey, come sit here." I thought, "Are you crazy—inviting him to sit with us?" But Frank came over, and yes, he really was a nerd. But he laughed at my jokes. Frank sat with us at our lunch table for the rest of middle school and even into high school.

When I think of bullying, I think of Frank, but I also think of Ryan. I think of how each one broke a certain kind of silence. Frank cried out, and Ryan quietly showed him real kindness.

Perhaps the easiest way to figure out if someone is your friend is if he doesn't laugh at you when you are hurt or humiliated or doesn't make you do something you don't want to do. A friend is someone you can hang out with and laugh with, but he or she also sticks up for you.

In Judaism, when you make a covenant or pact with someone, you make an agreement that you have each other's backs. Despite all the programs against bullying that exist in schools, no one can really completely protect you. But if you are a real friend to someone and he is to you, then you have someone with whom you have loyalty and trust.

The Hebrew word for a pact of friendship is *b'rit*. Religiously, this word is used for the covenant between God and the Jewish people, but it also has the more everyday meaning of a true friendship. If you have a *b'rit* with someone, you mean what you say, and you are there when you are needed. Even though you can really annoy each other at times, you get through arguments and make sure you can trust each other.

Sometimes men bond with each other, especially if they have faced adversity. A teammate on a sports team, your partner in a debate club, or a study partner is someone you have to rely on. You have to trust each other in order to succeed. In extreme situations, such as in a military unit, a team fighting for a championship, astronauts in a spaceship, or a high-pressure job, guys can get very close to each other because they have been through a lot together. Men call these kinds of friends "brothers." This isn't a biological brother who happens to be born into the same family with you. These are the brothers we make for ourselves. Having brothers is the opposite of the culture of cruelty we experience so often.

We have to stand up to cruelty by including others in our circle of brothers. No outside school program can do this for you. Every guy needs a brother.

"How good it is, and how pleasant, when brothers sit together" (Psalm 133:1).

"For my brothers' and friends' sakes, I say, 'Peace be with you'" (Psalm 122:8).

—RABBI JOSEPH

Find Yourself a Friend: Teen Voices

"You know when someone is really your friend when you know you can trust the person and he cares and doesn't laugh even when something embarrassing happens to you and everyone else is laughing."

"Guys fight, but an hour later we can forget about it, and we just start hanging out and playing sports. Girls hang onto grudges much longer than guys do."

"One of my best friends is a really funny guy. We joke around a lot, but when things need to be serious, we get serious. I don't remember the exact details, but one day I was over at his house and he couldn't be serious. I'm not sure if I had asked him something and he made a joke out of it or what happened. I remember being really mad and not talking to him for a while. Eventually the whole thing seemed stupid and we made up."

"No one really makes fun of us for being Jewish, but my Jewish friends and I kind of have a Jewish alliance."

"You know someone is your friend when you can talk to him about your problems."

" I think it's okay if friends pull pranks or tease you as long as you and they are both aware that nothing is meant by it. My friends and I know when to stop, and that's what's important."

"You know when someone is really your friend when he doesn't care how weird you are and he is consistently nice to you."

" People on my basketball team will pick on each other and push each other into walls, but we understand it is just part of a joke, not bullying, and may give them a little shove back."

"I sold something of mine to a friend with the promise that he would pay me the full amount the next day. He didn't have the money, and I ended up pestering him for three months about it. He finally paid me back. It was very annoying. He kept on moving the date further and further back."

" I think it is okay if friends pull pranks or tease you as long as you and they are both aware that nothing is meant by it."

"My friends at camp were getting together a couple of nights and purposefully excluded me just to make me mad. I was mad. I cried."

"Two people pretended to be friends with me so they would get invited to my bar mitzvah. Now we don't even talk. They never said one word to me at all after my party."

"Sometimes I walk through the halls at school and see stuff. If I speak up, am I a snitch? How will my friends trust me?"

"Bullying is not the issue. I don't understand why adults focus so much on bullying. It might happen—especially online—but the real issues are intolerance and indifference."

"In middle school, the eighth graders were cruel on my bus: lots of physical stuff, throwing around our books, backpacks, etc. As an eighth grader now, I make sure not to make the same mistake."

Did You Know?

Today, most people stay connected through social media, and we text each other constantly. The benefits are huge. You are able to share and laugh with friends. Everyone can wish you "happy birthday" on your birthday—even friends from camp or from a place you used to live. Photos and videos take seconds to share. You are able to talk all the time, whenever you want, to the people who matter to you. You are always connected. The negatives, however, are real, too.

Unfortunately you probably have had some experience with this. A momentary angry word is now permanently out there. People can manipulate what you type when they forward it so that it isn't true. Someone always has a camera to take a video when you are doing something embarrassing or not at your best. It is easy to use social media to humiliate someone. The Rabbis teach that someone who humiliates another person in public is committing a form of violence (*Bava Metzia* 58b). And every text or posting on the Internet is public. Like all tools, social media can be used for good or bad. It takes wisdom and maturity to be able to take a breath before you text or post something. As with all things, kindness and thoughtfulness should be your guides. Rabbi Menachem Mendel of Kotzk gave this advice: "Not everything that is thought should be said out loud, and not everything that is said out loud should be written, and not everything that is written should be published."[2]

✡ Joseph of the coat-of-many-colors fame was sold into slavery by his brothers because they resented that Joseph was their dad's favorite. They resented his dreams of superiority over them. Despite this evil act, many years later, after achieving success with the Pharaoh in Egypt, Joseph forgave his brothers and even supplied them with jobs and money. Now that's the ultimate demonstration of not holding a grudge.

✡ When you are between the ages of eighteen and twenty-six, if you are Jewish and have never traveled to Israel on a peer program, you can apply to visit Israel for free through a program called Taglit-Birthright Israel, funded by generous donors. What a great way to meet Jewish friends from all over the world! Almost four hundred thousand Jewish people from sixty-two countries have had this incredible opportunity. You have brothers (and sisters!) you didn't even know about.

⭐ During the time of the Soviet Union, most Jews living there were not allowed to emigrate or leave the country even for a short while. Jews were trapped behind the "Iron Curtain." To protest this unfairness, kids in America who had a bar/bat mitzvah would pair with a young person in the Soviet Union and have a bar/bat mitzvah with them symbolically.[3]

⭐ Keshet, a Jewish organization, works for inclusion of LGBTQ (lesbian, gay, bisexual, transgender, and queer and/or questioning) Jews in all facets of Jewish life—synagogues, Hebrew schools, day schools, youth groups, summer camps, social service organizations, and more. Keshet is led and supported by LGBTQ Jews and straight allies. Unfortunately, LGBTQs are too often the target of bullies. In some cases, gay guys have been beaten up or even murdered simply because they are gay.

Get Yourself a Teacher

Daniel Radcliffe

Friend to LGBTQ Youth

You know him as the seeker who scores the golden snitch for the Gryffindor team. But in real life, Daniel Radcliffe, the actor who played Harry Potter on-screen, doesn't need his Nimbus 2000 to make a difference in others' lives. Radcliffe was born in England to an Irish Protestant father and a Jewish mother who was born in South Africa and raised in England. While he is not an observant Jew, here's how he describes himself: "I think of myself as being Jewish and Irish ... [and] I am an atheist, but I am very proud of being Jewish."[4] Although many believe God is part of the foundation of Judaism, others do not have that belief and can identify with Daniel Radcliffe's point of view.

Taking a cue from the most famous character he has played thus far, Daniel uses his fame to be an advocate for people who are vulnerable. One of the many issues to which Radcliffe devotes his time and money is advocacy for LGBTQ teens who are at risk for discrimination and bullying. Radcliffe speaks out against homophobia, an unthinking dislike of homosexuals. He supports the Trevor Project, an organization that promotes awareness of gay teen suicide and urges the development of prevention techniques. In an interview with the *Telegraph*, a major newspaper in the United Kingdom, Radcliffe explains the importance of his choice:

> It is extremely distressing to consider that ... suicide is a top three killer of young people, and it's truly devastating to learn that LGBTQ youth are up to four times more likely to attempt suicide than [are] their heterosexual peers.... It's vitally important that young people understand they are not alone and, perhaps even more important, that their young lives have real value.[5]

David Axelrod

Friend to Israel

David Axelrod is the former senior White House adviser to President Barack Obama. In this role, David helped craft and communicate policies, including ones between the United States and Israel. While these two countries are allies, we also know allies don't always agree or like everything the other says or does. Expressing this very point at an Israel Independence Day address in Washington, DC, Axelrod said, "Let's not confuse the occasional dispute over policy with the fundamental relationship that has guided our two nations for so long and will continue to guide our two nations."[6] It is very important for all of us to consider which of our relationships are fundamental and can withstand problems and which will be broken if there is any dispute.

Micah Hendler

Friend of "the Enemy"

Micah Hendler is a lover of music and peace. He saw firsthand the power of music to bring together people with opposing perspectives. One of the ways to do this was to participate in Seeds of Peace, an international peace-building summer program that gives young people the opportunity to meet their historic enemies face-to-face. Every summer at the Seeds of Peace camp in Maine, teens from the Middle East, South Asia, and the United States enjoy traditional camp activities along with intense "mediated conflict resolution" sessions. Micah's experiences had a big impact on his life and motivated him to be what he calls a "musical peacemaker." He uses "music as a tool to bring people from different backgrounds, communities, and walks of life together to understand one another and work together for a better future."[7] In fact, Micah started the Jerusalem Youth Chorus in Israel to empower Jewish and Arab youth to become leaders in their communities and inspire singers and listeners around the world to work for peace.

Learn

Blood Brothers

> Jonathan's soul became bound up with the soul of
> David; Jonathan loved David as himself.... Jonathan and
> David made a pact [Hebrew: *b'rit*] because he loved him
> as himself. Jonathan took off the cloak and battle garb
> he was wearing and gave them to David, together with
> his sword, bow, and belt.
>
> **(1 Samuel 18:1–4)**

In this story, two soldiers—Jonathan and David—met during a
battle and began to rely on each other to protect each other's
lives. Jonathan saved David's life, and later David became king
of the Jewish people. Have you ever witnessed this kind of deep
friendship, or do you think this can occur only later in life? Here
are some more questions to consider.

- ✡ Why do you think men who are on the same team,
  whether it be debate, drama, sports, or something else,
  bond with each other?
- ✡ The Torah does not tell us what the pact between
  Jonathan and David consists of. What do you think
  it was? Jonathan gave David his sword, bow, and
  belt. What does it mean when you let someone
  else use your baseball glove, phone, or something
  similar that is important to you? Have you ever
  given someone something that was very meaningful
  to you, simply to show that person how strongly you
  feel about him?

⭐ Do you notice the word *b'rit* here, which we translate as "pact"? In what other context does the word *b'rit* or *bris* come up? How are the two situations connected?

⭐ Do you think that a *b'rit* between two boys is different from a *b'rit* between a girl and a boy who are good friends?

In the Heat of the Moment

Here's a change of pace from friendship and gifts. Let's talk about competition. Sometimes what starts out as friendly competition goes too far. In *The Chosen*, Chaim Potok's famous novel, two friends discuss what happened to them in the heat of the moment during a baseball game:

> "Do you know what I don't understand about that ball game? I don't understand why I wanted to kill you."
>
> I stared at him.
>
> "It's really bothering me."
>
> "Well, I should hope so," I said....
>
> "Do you remember I stood in front of the plate afterwards and looked at you?"
>
> "Sure." I remembered the idiot grin vividly.
>
> "Well, that's when I wanted to walk over to you and open your head with my bat."
>
> I didn't know what to say....
>
> "I can't figure it out. Anyway, I feel better telling you about it."[8]

⭐ Have you ever seen anybody act crazy or get into a fight over a game? What do you think of the rioting that sometimes takes place after some professional sports games?

✡ Do you think it was right for the boy in this excerpt from *The Chosen* to tell the boy that he wanted to kill him, or should he have kept this thought to himself?

✡ What would you have done if the guy who wanted to hit his friend on the head with his bat had told you what he had fantasized? Is this something that should be ignored? Reported? Discussed with someone else?

✡ Why do you think people get worked up over games and fight?

✡ After a fight is over, do you walk away and ignore it? Do you talk to the person? How do you make things right again?

What Do I Think?

Have you ever been really ticked off at a friend? Or have you been in a situation when you really threatened someone? Describe why and what you did about it.

_____

_____

_____

_____

_____

_____

Now for some questions that have intrigued people throughout history: How do you know when someone is really your friend? Are there different forms of friendship? Is one friend enough, or do you need many friends to feel good about yourself? Do you know how to be a good friend?

Many Jewish teenage boys go to summer camp
and have close "camp friends." Do you? If so,
what did you learn there? Has camp affected
your life in important ways?

_____

_____

_____

_____

_____

_____

_____

_____

_____

How important are your "friends" on Facebook
or some other kind of social network? Is it
important to have many? Why or why not?

_____

_____

_____

_____

_____

_____

_____

_____

_____

Explain a time you had to forgive a friend.
Describe a time when a friend has needed to
forgive you. Do you ever think about these things
on Rosh Hashanah and Yom Kippur, the times when
Jews are supposed to seek forgiveness from one
another? What does it feel like to apologize or
to receive an apology?

_____

_____

_____

_____

_____

_____

_____

_____

_____

Capture any of your additional thoughts or questions here.

_____

_____

_____

_____

_____

_____

_____

_____

_____

_____

Text Connection

וַיִּכְרֹת יְהוֹנָתָן וְדָוִד בְּרִית

Vayichrot Yonatan v'David b'rit.

Jonathan and David sealed a pact.

—1 Samuel 18:3

"Almost all people act one way when they are with a large group of people and act completely differently when they are with only a small group of friends."

"A kid in my grade was getting bullied. I wanted to speak up and say 'stop' but didn't. I will always remember that day in school."

True to myself

Sometimes things bother me, but I am not comfortable speaking up.

הָרִימִי בַכֹּחַ קוֹלֵךְ.…
הָרִימִי אַל־תִּירָאִי

Harimi vako'ach koleicha....
Harimi! Al tira'i!

Raise your voice with strength....
Lift it up! Do not be afraid!
—Isaiah 40:9

"Kids don't want to be called 'chicken' or other names. They also might not want to do drugs or drink, but other people are doing it, so they feel like they should or they won't be popular or cool."

"People feel that if they are cool, girls will like them, especially if they do what the tough, popular kids do."

True to Myself

Sometimes things bother me, but I am not comfortable speaking up.

Silence often feels safe. It may seem better not to say anything than to say something and feel stupid.

I was not the kind of kid who liked to be in the front of the class. I hated it when we had to give "oral reports," which meant standing up in front of the room and talking about whatever the assignment was. Once I had to get up in front of the class and talk about the Vikings. I had a poster (the required "visual aid") that I had to put in front of everyone. I stood in front of my snickering classmates and read my handwritten report. At one point, I had to point to my poster.

"Look, his hand is shaking," someone whispered.

I shot my hand back down to my side, kept my eyes glued to my paper, and read through the rest. When I finally sat down, I felt a mix of relief and embarrassment.

Who wants to get up in front of people and be humiliated? No one. But if everyone was silent because they were afraid of saying something stupid, what would that be like? What happens if the situation isn't as harmless as an oral report, but speaking up about something you see is wrong?

Many times guys feel pressure from their friends to keep quiet. They don't want to say anything that will make them feel embarrassed. Speaking up is standing out. It took me many years before I finally found my voice, before I finally spoke up about something that mattered to me.

My high school class decided to have a fund-raiser. They hired someone to come in and give us stuff to sell, and our class got a certain percentage of everything we sold. There were also prizes for the top sellers. The man they hired acted as if he was on a game show. If you sold $50 worth of merchandise, you got this. If you sold $100, you got that. And if you sold even more, you got to play "jumping for dollars."

"Jumping for dollars" was where the man took a roll of $10 bills, each bill taped end to end, and rolled them in a line across the cafeteria floor. Participants got to broad-jump as far as they could, and they got to keep whatever they jumped over.

Everyone was buzzing. People were talking about how far they could jump and how easily they could get hundreds of dollars. Apparently, as a motivator, it worked. People went out to sell their merchandise on behalf of the class.

I felt the whole thing was kind of stupid. How many people would really qualify for "jumping for dollars" anyway?

On my walk home from school that day, I passed the community center that I normally walked by without a thought. I happened to see some very poor people in line. You could tell they were poor by their clothes and how dirty they looked. Maybe they were getting groceries.

When I got home, I started thinking. I thought about $10 bills on the cafeteria floor and people jumping over them, playing a game. And I thought of the poor people standing in line. I decided to write a letter to the teacher who was the adviser to the school committee.

I don't remember exactly what I wrote, but it was something about how maybe we shouldn't be playing games with money.

I pictured the poor people watching us through the window while kids "jumped for dollars" and how they might feel. If we were going to raise money, shouldn't we do it in a better way and maybe give some of it to charity?

I was a bit nervous handing in my letter. I did not like to stand out, and I certainly didn't want to stand up and speak out to my entire high school class. To my surprise, a couple of teachers stopped me in the hallway and said, "I liked your letter." And then it was reprinted in the student paper.

It was a scary thing to speak up and somewhat easier to express myself only in a letter. But Judaism teaches us that when we care, we should say something. We shouldn't just go with the flow and do whatever everyone else is doing, even if our conscience says it's wrong. We have a long tradition of prophets, rabbis, and politicians who said that just because something is "normal" or "popular" doesn't make it right.

Judaism teaches us that we have two impulses, one for good (*yetzer hatov*) and one for bad (*yetzer hara*). Think of the classic angel on one shoulder and devil on the other. The bad impulse sometimes tells us just to lay low, be quiet, and not stand up or stand out. But we all also have a good impulse within us. It is our conscience or moral compass, our inner GPS. Some call it the voice of our soul.

Finding the inner voice and speaking up for others and for ourselves is difficult and demanding. Sometimes we don't have the words to say how we feel, and we sound so stupid to ourselves when we try to talk. But Judaism teaches that each person has a soul with a voice. We just have to learn to trust it and let it talk. Our *yetzer hatov* is real, and we have to learn to listen to it and let it speak. It is the voice of our higher selves, the way we were meant to be.

Judaism is telling each of us: trust yourself. Don't let yourself get trampled or your voice silenced. Don't be intimidated by any group or just go along with what everyone is saying. You have a moral core. That's who you really are.

Raise up your voice.

—**RABBI JOSEPH**

Find Yourself a Friend: Teen Voices

"Kids give in to peer pressure because they want to be popular and fit in. They make bad decisions. In the end, some kids aren't even accepted into the group because they were just being tricked by the popular kids."

"Almost all people act one way when they are with a large group of people and act completely differently when they are with only a small group of friends."

"When it comes to standing out or fitting in, kids who stay on both ends of the spectrum tend to get scrutinized. If you are extremely shy, people will make fun of you. Likewise, if you are boastful, cocky, or a jerk trying to stand out, people will also make fun of you."

"I wish I spoke up when my friend's lunch was pushed on the ground by a bully and no one did anything about it."

"A kid in my grade was getting bullied.
I wanted to speak up and say
'stop' but I didn't. I will always
remember that day in school."

"It is easier to ride the social current to the
top. Trying to fit in means trying to suppress
your personality to seem like other people
and keeping everything bottled up inside.
Being yourself, though, can make people point
and laugh as well. This is even worse."

"I think most kids want to fit in.
If you stand out, you risk being
judged. A common thought is that
different is weird and weird is bad."

"Kids don't want to be called 'chicken' or
other names. They also might not want to
do drugs or drink, but other people are
doing it, so they feel like they should
or they won't be popular or cool."

"Most of the time I don't speak up
in class. I feel comfortable with my
friends and family, but when most of my
classmates aren't my close friends, I
get nervous. I get scared that if I get
anything wrong, I will be judged for it. Even
though I know speaking up will benefit
me, I don't do it because of fear."

"People feel that if they are cool, girls will like them, especially if they do what the tough, popular kids do."

"Honestly, I wouldn't participate in tripping someone or doing something mean like that, but I wouldn't speak up against it, either."

Did You Know?

⭐ You probably know the story of Mordechai and Haman. But now, pause and consider how brave Mordechai must have been when Haman was walking down the street and everyone was bowing down to him. Mordechai refused to bow down. He literally risked his life to stand up to Haman publicly. It must have taken unbelievable strength of character to remain standing.

⭐ Although the Mordechai incident took place long ago, there are many examples of speaking up and standing out nowadays. Especially famous is "the Tank Man," or the "Unknown Protester," nicknames of an anonymous man who stood in front of a column of Chinese tanks the morning after the Chinese military forcibly removed protesters from Beijing's Tiananmen Square on June 5, 1989. By standing in front of the tanks, the "Unknown Protestor" stopped their advance.

⭐ According to *The Book of Lists* (2005), the greatest fear people have is not of death, disease, or spiders but of public speaking. We can be more afraid of exposing our true selves and being embarrassed than even of physical pain. Shame is more of a deterrent than just about anything.

⭐ In the Torah, we are instructed to listen to our conscience. In 1 Kings 3:12, God speaks to Solomon in his dream, encouraging him to follow his inner voice: "I have given you a wise and understanding heart...."

⭐ One of the most important contemporary Jewish heros is Natan Sharansky, who defied the entire Soviet political establishment despite his fears. He is one of the most famous "refuseniks," that is, a Jewish person who was refused permission to leave the Soviet Union. In 1978, Sharansky was convicted of treason and spying for the United States, because he worked undercover to try to smuggle Jewish people out of Russia. He was sentenced to thirteen years in a forced labor camp. However, Sharansky claims that once he discovered his Jewish roots, he was no longer a slave to the Soviet system and felt freer than ever before. Today he is an Israeli politician, author, and human rights activist.[1]

Get Yourself a Teacher

Howie Mandel

Speaking Up about Mental Health

It's not easy to share feelings of inadequacy—especially when you're a public figure whose life is in the media. But that's just what Howie Mandel, the well-known game show host of *Deal or No Deal* and TV, film, and stage actor, did in his autobiography.

He writes frankly about how his struggles with mysophobia (an out-of-control fear of germs that, among other things, keeps him from shaking hands) and other problems. In his book and on talk shows, he has discussed his ongoing struggles with obsessive-compulsive disorder (OCD), a condition in which someone does things—sometimes very strange things—over and over to avoid becoming anxious. People with OCD have a sense that if they take control of this seemingly meaningless behavior, disaster will be avoided. Mandel also suffers from attention deficit hyperactivity disorder (ADHD). This mental health problem can be seen in someone who cannot pay attention or control the impulse to speak, walk around, or make distracting sounds. Mandel opens up about his mental health challenges in an interview in *Ability Magazine*:

> I don't remember a time when I didn't feel there was an issue. But, I wasn't diagnosed until adulthood. I have always felt a little bit different, and I always knew I wasn't as comfortable with life as everybody else seemed to be.... When I was a kid, I didn't know anybody who went to a psychiatrist. There was always a stigma attached to mental health issues. But now I am taking care of myself ... and I am getting therapy.[2]

Daniel Smith

Speaking Up about Anxiety

Daniel Smith is a Jewish man who has written the book *Monkey Mind: A Memoir of Anxiety*. This book is full of interesting ideas, one of which is his analysis of Philip Roth's early short story "Eli, the Fanatic." In the story, a young suburban lawyer gets a case. It becomes his job to evict the tenants of a Hasidic yeshiva. Instead, Smith writes,

> he ends up wearing the "uniform" of the chief rabbi, wide-brimmed hat, phylacteries [tefillin], and all. Everyone thinks Eli has had a nervous breakdown, but, Roth writes, "he felt those black clothes as if they were the skin of his skin ... he would walk forever in that black suit, as adults whispered of his strangeness and children made 'Shame ... shame' with their fingers."[3]

Daniel Smith was thrilled by the uncompromising nature of Roth's characters. He loved their defiance in the face of shame. He exalted in their exceeding honesty—"even ... at the expense of their own serenity."[4] Standing up in this way takes very strong character.

Franz Rosenzweig

Speaking Up to Reclaim His Identity

Franz Rosenzweig (1886–1929) was a German soldier who fought in World War I. Although born to Jewish parents, he was raised with no Jewish education. It comes as no surprise that he didn't think of himself as a Jew. Nevertheless, Rosenzweig experienced unending antisemitism, leading him to conclude that being Jewish hampered his life. Soon, he reached the conclusion that it was best for him to convert to Christianity. Before converting, he decided to attend his first Yom Kippur service. What happened there shook his soul to such an extent that he made a private pledge to learn as much about Judaism as he could. Committed to his newfound identity, Rosenzweig gave up a promising secular academic career in order to live and teach in the Frankfurt Jewish community. Franz Rosenzweig went on to write *The Star of Redemption*, an important book of Jewish philosophy.

Learn

Pick Someone Else!

> Moses said to God, "Who am I to go to Pharaoh that I shall take the Children of Israel out of Egypt?" God replied, "I shall be with you, and this shall be the sign that I have sent you: When you take the people out of Egypt, you will serve God on this mountain" ... Moses said to God, "But they will not believe me and they will not listen to me.... Please, my Lord, I am not a man of words.... Send someone else!"
>
> **(Exodus 3:11–12, 4:1, 4:10, 4:13)**

Moses did not start off as a strong leader with a big voice. When God calls to him from a burning bush and commands him to go down to Egypt and tell Pharaoh to "let My people go," Moses flinches. "Who am I to go?" he says. "They won't listen to me or believe me, and I am not good with words." God tells him to go anyway. The rest is history.

- What are some of the objections Moses has to God's choosing him?
- Why is it hard to speak up? What is Moses (or anyone else) afraid of?

⭐ What could God have said to give Moses more confidence?

⭐ When do you feel confident? When don't you? What can you do to be more confident?

Finding Good, Finding Confidence

You have to judge everyone generously. Even if you have reason to think that person is completely rotten, it's your job to look hard and seek out some bit of goodness, some place in that person where he or she is not bad....

So now, my clever friend, now that you know how to think of people who seem bad and find some bit of good in them, do it for yourself as well!... Stay far, far away from sadness and depression.... I know what happens when you start looking at yourself: "Nothing good at all!" you think.... "Even the good things I did," you say, "were all for the wrong reasons. Impure motives! Lousy deeds!" But somewhere inside of you there is indeed a little bit of good.... Show yourself that is who you are.... It's that first dot of goodness that's the hardest to find (or the hardest to admit you found). The next ones will come a little easier, each one following another. And you know what? These little dots of goodness in yourself— after a while you will find that you can sing them and they become your song, the song you fashion by not letting yourself be pushed down and by rescuing your own good spirit from all that darkness and depression. The song can bring you to life.... (Rabbi Nachman of Breslov, *Likutei Moharan* 1:282)[5]

Rabbi Nachman is a very popular Hasidic hero from the nineteenth century. With these words, Rabbi Nachman is teaching us that just as we have to find the good in others, we also have to find the good in ourselves! Finding that good is what gives us confidence to be true to ourselves and avoid making bad decisions.

- When do you feel down or depressed?
- What do you do to make yourself feel better when you are feeling down?
- Over the past week, what is something good that you did? Focus on that good thing. That is who you really are!
- Music can help us find our voice. Rabbi Nachman teaches that each of us has our own song that comes from our "higher selves." What song or piece of music means a lot to you? Why?

What Do I Think?

Describe a time when you didn't speak up and wish you had.

_____

_____

_____

_____

_____

_____

_____

_____

_____

_____

Why do you think kids often give in to peer pressure?

_____

_____

_____

_____

_____

_____

_____

_____

_____

_____

_____

_____

Do you think most kids want to stand out or fit in? Why?

_____

_____

_____

_____

_____

_____

_____

_____

_____

_____

Capture any of your additional thoughts or questions here.

_____

_____

_____

_____

‑‑

‑‑

‑‑

‑‑

‑‑

Text Connection

הָרִימִי בַכֹּחַ קוֹלֵךְ...
הָרִימִי אַל־תִּירָאִי

Harimi vako'ach koleicha.... Harimi! Al tira'i!

Raise your voice with strength....
Lift it up! Do not be afraid!

—Isaiah 40:9

"Parents are clueless because they think I should get straight As, but they never did."

"I'm not popular, and my parents try to encourage me to do things that were popular when they were young—like bring a Walkman to school."

One day, son, this will all be yours

I love my parent(s), but adults can be clueless.

בִּטָּחוֹן

Bitachon

Trust

"When my parents ask how I am doing and I answer, 'Good,' it doesn't necessarily mean I'm doing good. I just want to be left alone."

"Parents make things worse by over-caring. I am so tightly packed in a bubble that I could suffocate."

One Day, Son, This Will All Be Yours

I love my parent(s), but adults can be clueless.

At some time during my teenage years, I moved into the basement of our house.

"I need my space," I declared, and the truth is, I did. My parents divorced when I was fourteen, my dad moved across town, my stepdad (who turned out to be a wonderful guy) arrived at around age sixteen, high school upped the homework and social pressure, and I needed some room to myself. Or, more specifically, I needed room away from my mom.

My mother was and is a loving, caring woman. There was nothing she would not do for me as I was growing up. But what I longed for most as a teenager was some privacy. I didn't need adults snooping over my shoulder, getting into my business.

The basement was great. There was a television if I wanted it. I had my own phone line. I could hear someone coming down the stairs. But more important, I was away from the noise of parental talking, incredibly boring gossip, and incessant questions about my life.

Let's face it, on my more frustrated or immature days, I didn't appreciate my parents at all. Sometimes adults can seem clueless. They would say things like, "Wait until you have some real responsibility." They seemed to have no idea how much stress I was really under.

"Have you completed your homework? When will you be home? What happened today in school?" They were all worry and no trust.

Not only that, but when I was feeling angry, I thought my parents were hypocrites. They lectured about being responsible, but sometimes they didn't seem so responsible themselves. There seemed to be a real double standard. For instance, they lectured me about drinking, but the first thing they did when they came home was have a drink. Were they that much more responsible just because they were older? And they talked about working hard, holding a job, getting good grades, but what were they really like when they were teens?

It is completely understandable that any thinking teenage guy would sometimes want to get away from, or at least not want to talk to, his parent or parents. It's natural to think it's better to talk to friends, who at least understand where you're coming from and what you're going through.

The fact may be, however, that the problem isn't that parents are clueless. The problem may actually be that they know too much. They think of all the stupid things they did when they were teens, and they are thankful and often lucky to have survived. And they are afraid you won't be so lucky. They may not be clueless; they may be scared.

Yes, they may even be hypocrites: they did things they shouldn't have done when they were teens. And, looking back, they know that part of your brain isn't fully developed, making you more impulsive and ready to take risks, especially in groups. Your brain has weak brakes when it comes to impulses.

Everyone is scared you are going to crash, no matter what you say or what promises you make. When you were a small child, you knew what it was like to be terrified. You forget that feeling as a teenager. You relearn the feeling as a parent.

Parents try to remember to be patient, encouraging, and loving while setting healthy boundaries and giving guidance for the unknown. They also know that you have to learn from your mistakes. They do better sometimes than others. And as for fear and trust, everyone has his ups and downs. At the end of the day, you are a son, no matter what.

Judaism talks about the obligations of a child to a parent. These obligations are so important that they became the fourth of the Ten Commandments. The Torah says that children owe their parents "honor" and "reverence" (Exodus 20:12 and Leviticus 19:3). But Judaism says there are also things kids deserve from their parents. The Talmud says parents owe their children an education and training in survival skills (*Kiddushin* 29a).

But underneath these obligations is a value that both parents and teens need to learn: *bitachon*, which means "trust," "faith," or "security." Do we have faith in each other? Faith in ourselves?
—**RABBI JOSEPH**

Find Yourself a Friend: Teen Voices

" Parents mean well but make things worse by asking too many questions or pushing a subject too hard. Like my brother doesn't know who he is going to prom with yet, and my mom is constantly aggravating him by pushing the fact that he doesn't have a date."

"I'm not popular, and my parents try to encourage me to do things that were popular when they were young— like bring a Walkman to school."

"My parents just don't understand how much drugs there are in school. I don't think they understand the pressure with drugs. If I wanted to, I could easily go and get high, but I choose not to."

"Parents are clueless because they think I should get straight As, but they never did."

"Just the other day my mom stole my phone and went looking through my texts and Facebook. It's like she doesn't have any trust in me."

"Every day when I get home from school my parents ask me how my day was, and I reply, 'Fine.' Then they say, 'Why don't you ever say anything about school?' I answer, 'I don't want to talk about it.'"

"I think that my parents trust me with everyday decisions but are not sure if I can handle important ones."

"When my parents ask how I am doing and I answer good, it doesn't necessarily mean I'm doing good. I just want to be left alone."

"Parents don't understand peer pressure. My parents don't realize the stress that the people in my grade have. There's also school, which makes me tired and stressed."

" Any time I have a story from school in which I did something and got yelled at, they are like I did something so terrible. You would think I had been arrested or something."

"Parents mean well but make things worse by attempting to give me advice. Whether it is relationships, school, or basketball, they always tell me to be a leader and put myself out there, but sometimes you have to be the quiet, laid-back kid."

" When have my parents been clueless? Their entire lives!!! Ninety-nine percent of arguments where I clearly have more or better points than they do, I still don't 'win.' For example, my parents won't let me have video games rated 'M' for mature."

"Parents make things worse by overcaring. I am so tightly packed in a bubble that I could suffocate."

" They mean well but make things worse by calling the house of the party I'm going to, to ensure parents will be present. I know they don't want me to be at an unattended party, but calling the house or e-mailing the mom is ridiculous."

"My mom asks what I got for a grade
on the test the same day I take it!"

"When my parents ask how I am
doing and I answer, 'Good,' it doesn't
necessarily mean I'm doing good.
I just want to be left alone."

"My dad is really tech-savvy, so I don't get
away with too much on the Internet."

Did You Know?

🌟 People have long discussed the fourth commandment,
"Honor your father and your mother" (Exodus 20:12).
Are there circumstances when it is does not apply?
Do children have to earn their parents' love, and do
parents have to earn their children's respect? When
people relate to each other in a positive way regardless
of their behavior, we are talking about "unconditional
love." That is the kind of love the commandment is
referring to, even though it does not use the Hebrew
word for "love," *ahavah*.

🌟 Ben Stiller, star of *Night at the Museum* and other
popular movies, began his TV career with his own
comedy show on MTV. He followed in the footsteps
of his mom and dad, both of whom were actors, and
he has included his parents in various episodes. Ben
Stiller seems to honor his parents a great deal.

⭐ Lender's Bagels (you've seen them in the frozen-food section of the supermarket) was a family business for over fifty years. A Jewish baker from Poland, Harry Lender, came to the United States and got his start in a bagel bakery in New Jersey. From there he launched his own business and ultimately passed it on to his sons. Thanks to the Lender family, today people of all faiths enjoy defrosted bagels far and wide. Not all sons (and daughters) make good business partners with the earlier generation, but when it works well, it's great. Could you imagine going into business with your parent(s) one day?

⭐ Do you know any stay-at-home dads? Do you think that because they are not working outside the house, they will have a unique relationship with their children? *Wikipedia* says the following about stay-at-home dads:

> It is becoming more important and more advantageous for men to establish fulfilling relationships with their children. They are beginning to value these relationships over financial gains. A survey conducted by Minnesota's Department for Families and Children's Services shows that men consider child care to be far more important than a paycheck. Of 600 dads surveyed, a majority said their most important role was to "show love and affection" to kids. "Safety and protection" came next, followed by "moral guidance," "taking time to play," and "teaching and encouraging." "Financial care" finished last. Many men are now becoming more involved in their children's lives, and be-

cause of that many men now have a better understanding of what life is like for their child growing
up in modern society.[1]

⭐ Leading causes of death are different depending on
your age. Are you surprised to learn that the leading
cause of death for American teens is car crashes, which
account for more than one-third of all teen deaths?
Some of these teenagers were passengers; in other
cases, the teens were driving, and of these, almost
20 percent were distracted by cell phone use. Your
parent(s) may not know these exact statistics, but they
know that in general teenagers are not good drivers.
They probably know this because they were teens once.
Do these statistics give you a new perspective on what
might seem like incessant nagging from your parents
to drive carefully?

Get Yourself a Teacher

Adam Sandler

Nephew

Undoubtedly Adam Sandler's movies and songs make you
laugh. How many times have you cracked up at his song about
Hanukkah? Rhyming it with "Veronica"? And "harmonica"?

As a kid, Adam entertained his friends, classmates, and
family, too, and, as you might suspect, he crossed the line a few
times too many. His uncle Mike writes in a post on Sandler's
website, "I love you doing what you do. It always reminds me

of the times in your living room in New Hampshire and you entertaining the family. Of course I also remember your father chasing you down the hall ... for being such a goof ball. But, now goof ball is a good thing. Even though I am sure, if your dad was around he would still be ... chasing you down some hallway."[2]

As with many kids, Adam's rowdy childhood antics often upset his family, but his family stuck by him, just as Sandler sticks by his family today. How many stars would invite their uncles to write on their websites?

Avrom Honig

Grandson

It's easy to dismiss elders for being out of touch. They don't know the latest expressions or how to use today's gadgets. But who makes the best matzah balls? Who can tell you which teams won the World Series in '67, '73, and '99? And, most important, who loves you through thick and thin?

Avrom Honig is a television producer. When he needed to create a demo reel to land his first job in film production, whom did he video? His grandmother, whom he calls "Bubbe," Yiddish for "grandmother." That launched Bubbe on a new career herself as the chef in their cooking show, *Feed Me, Bubbe*, and started Avrom on his TV career.

As the *Wall Street Journal* newspaper reported about this unexpected collaboration for both of them, "'It is a great opportunity for us to spend time together and to share recipes for the future,' says Ms. Sher, who is in her eighties. For Mr. Honig, it offers a chance to showcase his grandmother's tasty cooking and zestful personality: 'I get to share the wonderful feelings Bubbe gives me ... with the world.'"[3] While it's clear that Bubbe has helped her grandson, Avrom has given his grandmother and grandfather (his production assistant) the gift of new experiences, appreciation, and respect. Bubbe may not be able to text, but boy can she cook.

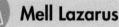

Mell Lazarus

Son

Mell Lazarus created the comic strip *Momma* in 1970. The strip has been syndicated for over forty years and currently appears in more than four hundred newspapers worldwide. When Lazarus first showed the comic strip to his mother, she replied, "You caught Aunt Helen to a tee!" While his own mother was his inspiration, Lazarus points out that *Momma* reflects everyone's mother. An important underlying message in all of his strips: do not write off a mother's good intentions, for even if she is annoying, she is still on your team. Maybe that's why the strip has stood the test of time. *Momma* has been giving us motherly advice for decades.

Learn

Here I Am

God said to Abraham, "Take your son, your one-and-only, whom you love, Isaac, and go to the land of Moriah. Offer him up there on one of the mountains I will show you." Abraham got up early in the morning, saddled his donkey, cut wood for the sacrifice, and went out to the place of which God had told him.... Abraham took the wood of the burnt offering and laid it upon Isaac his son. He took the fire in his hand, and a knife, and both of them went together. Isaac then spoke to Abraham his father, and said, "My father," and he said, "Here I am, my son." He said, "Here are the fire and the wood, but where is the lamb for a burnt offering?" Abraham said, "God will see to the lamb for a burnt offering, my son." And both of them went together.

(Genesis 22:2–3, 6–8)

Abraham believes he has been commanded to sacrifice his son. He obeys. He does not tell his son, Isaac, where they are going. Very little is said on the way of what must have felt like a very long three-day journey. In the end, God keeps Abraham from sacrificing his son, saying it was a test of faith.

- ✡ How are Abraham and Isaac each feeling in this story?
- ✡ Why doesn't Abraham tell Isaac more about what is happening?
- ✡ Why does the story repeat the phrases "my father" and "my son"? What does this do to the drama of the story?
- ✡ The dialogue and journey begin with a description of Abraham and Isaac going off together and end with the phrase "both of them went together." What is ironic about this phrase?
- ✡ When do you have the most meaningful conversations with your parent(s)? What questions would you like to ask them?
- ✡ Today, people risk their lives when they enlist in the military. Can you think of other times you would risk yourself for something you believe in?

In My Father's Shadow

Rabbi W. Gunther Plaut has this to say about the story of Abraham and Isaac:

> Even as God is the dominant Father and Abraham a trusting and obedient son, so in the purely human realm does Abraham appear as the dominant father and Isaac as ... the submissive son. Only once does Isaac speak and ask the fateful question; thereafter he is a mere object of the drama. Abraham, the ... patriarch, the honored and aged friend of God, overawes his timid son, whose will to independence may well have been crippled by doting and protective parents.... In a way all parents seek to dominate their children and are in danger of seeking to sacrifice them to parental plans or hopes.[4]

- Do you sometimes feel that you are being "sacrificed" to your parents' "plans or hopes"?
- What do you think is the effect the near sacrifice of Isaac has on his future relationship with his father?
- Psychologist Sam Osherson claims that many men suffer from "father hunger," which is the need to know who our father really was and how he felt during his childhood. Does this make sense to you? Why or why not?
- Some men have been raised to believe that they should be unemotional with their children, particularly their sons. In most cases, children with fathers such as these developed their own difficulties in communicating. Can you imagine why?

Roles and Role Models

Honor your father and your mother.
                    (Exodus 20:12)

Revere your mother and your father.
                    (Leviticus 19:3)

The Talmud (*Kiddushin* 30b–31a) says that for "revere," the mother is stated first to make up for the fact that we naturally tend to revere our fathers more. For "honor," the father is stated first because we naturally tend to honor our mothers more in that they are the ones we can talk to.

> Our Rabbis taught: What is "revere" and what is "honor"? "Revere" means that he [the son] must neither stand nor sit in his [the father's] place, nor contradict his words, nor argue against him. "Honor" means that he must give his father food and drink, clothe and give him shoes, and help him go in and out.
>
> **(Talmud, *Kiddushin* 31b)**

⭐ The Talmud notices a change in the word order of the Torah when it comes to mothers and fathers. The first parent is named to make up for a natural imbalance. Do you think it is true that mothers are the ones sons can talk to more easily? Do you think it is true that sons naturally revere or fear their fathers? Why or why not?

⭐ The Rabbis understand "revere" as respecting and not embarrassing a father. Do you think this holds true for today? When might a parent feel embarrassed? When does your parent embarrass you?

⭐ Have you ever been told not to sit in someone's seat because it "belongs" to the father and grandfather? When did that happen?

⭐ How do you express your love for your parents?

⭐ The Rabbis interpret "honor" for when your parents are older and you might have to take care of them. Can you imagine being in that position? How might you handle it?

⭐ Many people say that we act in ways similar to how our parents acted when they were kids. Do you think this will be true of you? In what ways? In what ways not?

Paternal Job Description

The father is bound in respect of his son: to circumcise, redeem, teach him Torah, take a wife for him, and teach him a craft. Some say, to teach him to swim too.

(Talmud, *Kiddushin* 29a)

In the Rabbis' time, people believed that fathers raised sons, while mothers raised daughters.

⭐ What do you think of the Talmud's list of obligations of a father to a son? What is surprising? What, in your opinion, is missing?

Each of these actions is supposed to be understood both literally and symbolically:

⭐ "Circumcise": This means *b'rit milah*, but it also sometimes refers to a parent causing his or her child necessary pain. What pain do you think you have to suffer in order to grow?

✡ "Redeem": Traditionally, firstborn sons were supposed to serve in the Temple in Jerusalem. A father "redeemed" his baby boy when he reached thirty days of age by paying for him to be released from this obligation. Some people think that *pidyon haben,* the name of this ceremony, keeps the child from being overwhelmed with a task he cannot handle. When is a time your parent(s) kept you from doing something because you weren't ready?

✡ "Teach him Torah": In the Rabbis' time, this referred to all education. Is school something that is a source of agreement or conflict between you and your parent(s)? What about Hebrew or day school? The obligation to educate your son may be translated into the obligation to pay for college education or even for a graduate education like law school or medical school. When do you think the father's obligation ends?

✡ "Take a wife for him": We are long past the age of arranged marriages. But would you ever go to your parent(s) for advice on relationships?

✡ "Teach him a craft" and "teach him to swim": Contemporary parents eventually want you to be self-sufficient. What are some areas where you are more independent than you were a few years ago? In what areas do you imagine you will be more independent next year? When do you want a parent's help? When don't you?

What Do I Think?

Describe when your parents have been completely clueless.

_____

_____

_____

_____

_____

_____

_____

_____

_____

Complete the sentence: I know my parent(s) mean well, but sometimes they make things worse by ...

_____

_____

_____

_____

I want to be like my father in some ways but not in others, among them:

Some things that my parent(s) have done that
make me proud are:

_____

_____

_____

_____

_____

_____

_____

_____

Capture any of your additional thoughts or questions
here.

_____

_____

_____

_____

_____

_____

_____

_____

_____

_____

_____

_____

_____

_____

Text Connection

בִּטָחוֹן

Bitachon

Trust

"I can't explain God, but I can feel God."

"It doesn't matter if you believe in God because God nevertheless exists. It is more important to be a good person. I also believe in heaven."

God ... really?

I am not sure I believe in God because the world is pretty messed up.

שְׁמַע יִשְׂרָאֵל יְיָ אֱלֹהֵינוּ יְיָ אֶחָד

Sh'ma Yisrael: Adonai Eloheinu Adonai echad.

Listen, member of the people Israel: the Eternal is our God, the Eternal is one.
—Deuteronomy 6:4

"If there is a God, why would God let people die from natural disasters or other causes of death? How do people even know if there is a God with us?"

"I don't believe in God, but I still feel like I belong as a Jew. I feel connected with other people culturally. I also like the values encouraged in Judaism."

God ... Really?

I am not sure I believe in God because the world is pretty messed up.

A train is derailed, killing twenty people. A person who survives thinks, "Wow! God must have had another plan for me."

A group of tourists arrives at the Grand Canyon, stand on the edge, and look down. Its grandeur takes their breath away. At night, they return for a look at the night sky. Free of pollution, the stars shine above the awe-struck crowd. "God is an amazing artist," someone whispers.

An earthquake hits a small country, killing tens of thousands of people. People throw up their hands and say, "It's an act of God. There's nothing we could have done to prevent these people from dying."

A child is born. Her screams fill the halls of the hospital, and the parents weep tears of joy. They say, "Thank God our baby is healthy."

Down the hall, another baby is born, but with a severe birth defect. The child will probably not survive long. "Why is God doing this to me?" the mother asks. The father says, "I guess God needs another angel up in heaven."

The word "God" is used quite freely. "In God we Trust." God gets a lot of credit but also a lot of blame. There are times when we feel great awe and wonder, and we cannot help but think that something called "God" made it all possible. But there are other times, when we feel the suffering and pain of the world, when it is normal to think, "I am not sure I believe in God because the world is pretty messed up."

In Hebrew school, children are taught stories about God in the context of the Bible. Children are taught that God is "compassionate and gracious, slow to anger, abounding in kindness and faithfulness, extending kindness to the thousandth generation, and forgiving iniquity, transgression, and sin" (Exodus 34:6–7). But children are also taught that God smote the Egyptians with ten plagues and flooded the world when people acted wickedly. It is hard to reconcile these stories.

When we were children, we probably pictured God as an old man with a white beard sitting on a cloud. Research has shown that this is a very common way of depicting God.

We might also have been taught that God watches over us, rewards us for living according to the commandments, and punishes the wicked. It is no coincidence that childhood ideas of God picture God as a parent who keeps us safe but also disciplines us, because that is the way kids think. Eventually we learn to ask questions, such as why good people suffer or if life has meaning.

Part of growing up means that we can leave behind childhood notions and replace them with something more sophisticated. You may have faith in a personal God who rewards and punishes. But there are other Jewish definitions of God, such as the following:

1. While large parts of the Hebrew Bible talk about God as an old man or a warrior, other parts of the Bible describe God differently. Some prophets and the Song of Songs depict God as a friend or someone you love. We feel close to God, therefore, when we feel trust

and love for another human being. In the musical
Les Miserables, this concept is present in the idea that
"to love another person is to see the face of God." A
similar thought can be found in Genesis when Jacob is
reunited with his brother, Esau, after a long time and
after a bitter conflict. Jacob says, "To see your face is
like seeing the face of God" (Genesis 33:10).

2. Elijah the prophet (think Passover) was once frightened
   and ran away. The Bible says it was then that he heard
   a "still, small voice" (1 Kings 19:12). When he listened
   to that voice, he knew what he needed to do. For some,
   God is the feeling in their hearts about what is right
   and what is wrong. God as the "still, small voice"
   means God is our conscience.

3. Moses Maimonides (1135–1204), a Jewish thinker
   and student of Greek philosophy, wanted a rational
   understanding of God. He said that we could not
   understand what God is because God is higher than
   our minds can comprehend. Like the philosopher
   Aristotle, Maimonides wrote that God's thoughts
   are a higher truth beyond our understanding, "pure
   thought thinking itself" (*Mishneh Torah*, Foundations
   of the Torah 2:10). Other times he called God "the
   First Cause," or the reason the universe exists. Even if
   the logic or ultimate laws of the universe are beyond
   us, Maimonides claimed, nevertheless, God still
   communicates to us through the commandments and
   made a logical world with laws of nature.

4. Jewish mystics, or kabbalists, understood God as a
   power that permeates and surrounds the universe.
   God is like "the Force" in *Star Wars*. God is what unifies

everything because God is in everything and beyond. God is literally in you, your friend, the tree, the sky, and the stars. Some mystics claim that God is like the ocean, and we are like the waves. It appears that we are separate and distinct, but we are really part of something larger, bigger than we know.

You do not have to know all the answers or have it all figured out, but you also don't have to believe the same thing you used to believe when you were younger. You can change your mind when you are older. You are free to redefine the word "God." Jews have been doing so for centuries. *Sh'ma Yisrael*: "Listen, member of the people Israel: the Eternal is our God, the Eternal is one" (Deuteronomy 6:4). The main point is that you should not stop asking questions, and you don't have to accept someone else's definition of God that does not work for you.

—RABBI JOSEPH

[Note: When we talk about God, it is easy to fall into the habit of referring to God as "he." But we know that God is beyond gender. We should try to use language that points to God as not gendered.]

Find Yourself a Friend: Teen Voices

" I feel close to God when something really good or really bad happens."

"I don't believe in God, but I still feel like I belong as a Jew. I feel connected with other people culturally. I also like the values encouraged in Judaism."

" I think prayer is important because it gives people emotional and psychological help. If someone is praying for a sick person, it will make them feel better."

"I consider myself an atheist, but my parents won't let me. They still force me to go to temple and Hebrew school. The two main reasons I think this is because of science and just my way of thinking. God does not make one person suffer and save another's life. God doesn't choose to send natural disasters and is not 'Luck.' I understand why a lot of people do believe in 'God,' but it is not for me."

" I can't explain God, but I can feel God."

"I feel close to God or wishing God would be on my side when I have projects to do at the last minute or when it is overtime in a championship game. I feel close to God when I want something great to happen to me or when I don't want to do something even though I have to."

" It does not matter if you believe in God. What matters is who a person is. It matters who you are and what your values are."

" I think that often people are curious
and want an explanation for something,
so they give God credit or blame."

"I don't think it matters if you believe
in God, because you can still pray
and be thankful for things without
it going out to a specific being."

" I think prayer is important because
everyone needs to voice his or her wishes
and thanks at some point, and prayer is just
that. When you actually say something,
there is a better chance of it happening."

"I don't know if I have ever felt close
to God, considering I have a hard time
believing in God. I'm not saying I don't
believe in God. I do in my own way. I just
have never felt particularly close to God.
I feel far away from God whenever I
hear about a tragedy. Even if it doesn't
necessarily affect me, I just don't think
that a God that is as compassionate as God
is said to be would allow these things."

" It doesn't matter if you believe in
God because God nevertheless exists.
It is more important to be a good
person. I also believe in heaven."

" *If there is a God, why would God let people die from natural disasters or other causes of death? How do people even know if there is a God with us?*"

"*For people who are certain God exists, prayer is helpful because they know someone is listening to them.*"

" *There are more pressing matters than worrying about whether there is God. It is more important to me to take action and protest than it is to pray.*"

Did You Know?

⭐ There are many different Jewish beliefs concerning whether there is life after death. Jews have believed various things at different times throughout history. In the biblical period, Jewish people thought that when we die, we all go to a land of the dead called Sheol. In Rabbinic times, Jews believed righteous people will be resurrected. Later, during the Middle Ages, Jews believed that some of us will go to heaven and others to hell. Kabbalists and Jewish mystics believe we are reincarnated. A mainstream belief today is very uplifting. It maintains that while our body returns to the earth, our spirit goes to God, and our righteous deeds, or *mitzvot*, live on after us.

✡ Judaism is mostly a religion of *deed*, not *creed*. Judaism cares more about what you **do** (visiting the sick, giving *tzedakah*, celebrating holidays) than what you personally believe. Even though there are some beliefs that tradition considers to be commandments (to believe in only one God, to believe people are made in the divine image, not to worship idols), some people believe you can be an atheist (someone who does not believe in God) and still be Jewish. Famous Jewish people who called themselves atheists include Carl Sagan and Sigmund Freud.

✡ Different modern definitions of being a Jew exist in the world today. According to traditional Jewish law, or *halachah*, you are a Jew if you were born to a Jewish mother or have converted to Judaism. (Liberal and Reform branches of Judaism modified this idea to say you are a Jew if you were born to either a Jewish mother or father, as long as you are raised as a Jew.)[1] The State of Israel's definition of who is eligible for Israeli citizenship under the Law of Return is someone who had a Jewish parent or grandparent, is the spouse of a Jew, or has converted to Judaism under any denomination of Judaism. In essence, the State of Israel has created a national Jewish identity, and if you would have been persecuted as a Jew under the Nazis' antisemitic Nuremberg Laws, you are eligible to immigrate to the Jewish homeland.

✡ People often question how God can exist if there is evil in the world. But there is an important distinction we should make: *evil* is something human beings do to each other through their own free will (such as murder or stealing); *suffering* comes from the pain of living. In other words, when a lion attacks an animal or a virus attacks a person, it may be gruesome and unfair, but it is not evil. When people do harm to each other, people may ask, "Where is God?" But it is just as fair to ask, "Where is humankind?"

Contemporary rabbi Harold Kushner wrote *When Bad Things Happen to Good People* after his three-year-old son was diagnosed with a degenerative disease that would allow his son to live only until his early teens. Rabbi Kushner's book was a response to his own fears. In it, he shares his wisdom as a rabbi, a parent, a reader, and a human being. *When Bad Things Happen to Good People* has become a classic that offers clear thinking and consolation in times of sorrow. Since its original publication in 1981, it has brought solace and hope to millions of readers.

Get Yourself a Teacher

Emil Fackenheim

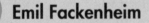

Honoring His Jewish Heritage

Just before the Holocaust, Emil Fackenheim (1916–2003) moved from Germany to Canada and then to Israel and managed to avoid the Nazis. He admitted it was hard to believe in God after the Holocaust. But he said that stopping being Jewish was like handing Hitler a victory after the fact. Even if the reason was yet to be discovered, Fackenheim said he felt commanded to survive as a Jew no matter what. After all, if Holocaust survivors could live after everything they had been through and still insist on being Jewish, shouldn't he?

Albert Einstein

Honoring a Force Grander Than Humankind

Albert Einstein's (1879–1955) contributions to the scientific world are immeasurable. His theory of relativity—that matter can be converted into energy ($E = MC^2$)—is perhaps the most famous formula of all time. Despite his brilliance and passion for science, he respected a life force beyond human comprehension, but not the traditional view of God as personal creator. He expressed this thought, captured by the *New York Times* in Einstein's obituary: "My religion consists of a humble admiration of the illimitable superior spirit who reveals himself in the slight details that we are able to perceive with our frail and feeble minds."[2]

Learn

My God and God of My Ancestors

The Baal Shem Tov taught: Why does our prayer begin with "Blessed are You, *Adonai*, my God and God of my ancestors, God of Abraham, God of Isaac," etc.? Because Abraham had his understanding of God, and Isaac had his, and so did each and every person. We say "my God" because we can have our own unique understanding of God, but we also say "God of my ancestors" because we need to link our faith to theirs. Our faith alone can change on any given day, but blind acceptance in the beliefs of others will not last. We need both.

- ✡ Why do you think it is important for each of us to have our own understanding of God?
- ✡ Why is it important to understand the faith of your ancestors?
- ✡ How did you understand God when you were a child? In a synagogue today? Out in the street in your regular life? How might you think of God in the future?

Author of the World

Bachya ibn Pakuda wrote that God as the Creator and Designer of the universe made sense to him. He proposed the situation of someone coming up to you with a piece of paper with writing on it and saying, "Guess what happened? I was sitting at my desk and I accidentally knocked over a bottle of ink. The ink spilled and made these words in these perfect lines that you can read." If that happened, taught Bachya, you would certainly laugh in his face and say that was impossible. But how much more subtle the design, the depth of meaning, and the incredible intricacy of the world compared to words on a piece of paper! Just as the writing implies an author, the world implies a Creator.

- ✡ What do you think of Bachya ibn Pakuda's proof of God? Is it convincing?
- ✡ Can you find any flaws in his argument?
- ✡ When you look at nature, do you think there is a design or purpose?

Traditional Beliefs

Maimonides made a list of what he felt were the thirteen most basic ideas of Judaism. In abbreviated form, the Thirteen Articles of the Jewish Faith proposed by Maimonides are as follows:

1. God exists.
2. God is one and unique.
3. God has no physical body.
4. God is eternal.
5. Prayer is to God only.
6. The prophets spoke truth.
7. Moses was the greatest of the prophets.
8. The Written and Oral Torah were given to Moses.
9. There will be no other Torah.
10. God knows the thoughts and deeds of everyone.
11. God will reward the good and punish the wicked.
12. The Messiah will come.
13. The dead will be resurrected.

Nevertheless, many people who call themselves Jewish either question or reject these ideas.

⭐ Do you think that people who don't believe all of these ideas should stop calling themselves Jewish? Why or why not?

⭐ If you were to make a list of the most important elements of Judaism, what would they be?

What Do I Think?

When do you feel close to God? When do you feel far away?

_____

_____

_____

_____

_____

_____

_____

_____

_____

_____

_____

_____

_____

Do you think it matters if you believe in God? Why or why not?

_____

_____

_____

_____

Do you think prayer is important? Why or why not?

Capture any of your additional thoughts or questions here.

_____

_____

_____

_____

_____

_____

_____

_____

_____

Text Connection

שְׁמַע יִשְׂרָאֵל יְיָ אֱלֹהֵינוּ יְיָ אֶחָד

Sh'ma Yisrael: Adonai Eloheinu Adonai echad.

Listen, member of the people Israel: the
Eternal is our God, the Eternal is one.

—Deuteronomy 6:4

"If you look closely at everything, you will be grateful, because life is truly miraculous."

"I love playing guitar. I am good at it, and it can lead to big life moments and opportunity. It makes me feel better than anything."

The Torah of everything

Now that I think I think about it, that's amazing!

מָה־רַבּוּ מַעֲשֶׂיךָ יְיָ כֻּלָּם בְּחָכְמָה
עָשִׂיתָ מָלְאָה הָאָרֶץ קִנְיָנֶךָ

Mah rabu ma'asecha Adonai!
Kulam b'chochmah asita;
mal'ah ha'aretz kinyanecha.

Adonai, You have made so much! In wisdom You have made them all; the Earth is full of Your creations.

—Psalm 104:24

"We have Jewish values— tzedakah, tikkun olam. But we are normal teens. We hang out with friends, we go to school, do our homework."

"When I play a sport, I always wear a mezuzah around my neck. It makes me feel that something is protecting me."

The Torah of Everything

Now that I think about it, that's amazing!

Everywhere you look you will find an opportunity for amazement.

Baseball

Consider the science behind pitching a baseball. Velocity, spin, and friction all combine to make it do amazing things. You can sit and enjoy an entire baseball game just watching a great pitcher be in the zone. And since baseball is one of the few games without a clock, it ends whenever it ends. Sports is often talked about in terms of winning, losing, or just having fun. But it could also be about seeking perfection: the perfect pass, the perfect catch, the most beautiful arc of a ball as it travels through the air.

Music

Music is a series of vibrations in the air. It follows certain laws and scales. If you hold a guitar up to another guitar that is tuned the same way and you pluck a string on one of them, the same string on the other guitar will also vibrate. This is called sympathetic vibration. In playing music, you are not just having fun or filling a requirement for school. You are engaging in an activity as ancient as humanity itself.

Mobile phones and computers

People regularly talk and text on their mobile phones. Consider for a moment that your voice goes out into outer space and then is relayed directly to the person you want to talk to, all at incredible speed. Think of that the next time you complain about your phone service! And even though computers are everyday tools (and we become aggravated when they crash or are infected with viruses), they are still what we use to compose literature and art.

Nature

When leaves fall from the trees, they die and begin to decay. From strict biological necessity, they should only go from green to brown. However, they change colors, not because they need to but because they are made that way.

The list of amazing experiences goes on and on. There is no question as to whether the world is stunning: it is. The question is whether we notice.

Many times, in order to feel amazement, we feel we have to go to great extremes. We see people jump out of a helicopter with a snowboard and go down a mountain. People climb into cages and feed sharks. Another person tries to get close to an active volcano.

Judaism is not about thrill-seeking highs. It is about seeing the extraordinary within the ordinary. Your everyday activities—sports, music, and computers, all of it—are actually miraculous when you think about them. This is why the Jewish prayer book quotes the book of Psalms, "*Adonai*, You have made so much! In wisdom You have made them all; the earth is full of Your creations" (Psalm 104:24).

Imagine if you were mindful enough to notice how amazing every day is. Would you be less inclined to take things for granted? Be more grateful? Have more patience?

Rabbi Abraham Joshua Heschel (1907–1972) was born in Poland and escaped to the United States just before the Holocaust. Although he lived decades ago, many people still find meaning in his words. He taught that we should feel "radical amazement" about the world. We shouldn't feel amazed only at seeing very special things, like the aurora borealis or Niagara Falls. We should also feel amazed at everyday moments, like enjoying a meal with our family, taking a deep breath of fresh air, and seeing the smile on our friend's face. Rabbi Heschel wrote:

> Mankind will not perish for want of *information*; but only for want of *appreciation*. The beginning of our happiness lies in the understanding that life without wonder is not worth living. What we lack is not a will to believe but a will to wonder.[1]

With these words, Rabbi Heschel is teaching us to "stop and smell the roses," or to appreciate the gift of just being alive. What the world needs is not necessarily more knowledge or technical know-how. What we need is to feel wonder. You and your world are amazing!

How can you live a life with more wonder? What is keeping you from doing so? Can you recognize this moment, right now as you are reading this, as a gift?

Sometimes Jewish people acknowledge the experience of amazement by saying blessings. One very famous blessing is the *Shehecheyanu*, which comes from the Hebrew word *chai*, or "life." The blessing goes:

בָּרוּךְ אַתָּה יְיָ אֱלֹהֵינוּ מֶלֶךְ הָעוֹלָם,
שֶׁהֶחֱיָנוּ וְקִיְּמָנוּ וְהִגִּיעָנוּ לַזְּמַן הַזֶּה.

Baruch atah Adonai Eloheinu Melech haolam, shehecheyanu v'kiy'manu v'higianu laz'man hazeh.

Blessed are You, *Adonai* our God, Ruler of the universe, who gives us life, sustains us, and enables us to reach this moment.

Traditionally, you can say this blessing for everything from celebrating holidays to wearing new clothes. Saying it means we stop and notice that everyday life is actually amazing.

Can you think of a time recently when you could say the *Shehecheyanu*?

—RABBI JOSEPH

Find Yourself a Friend: Teen Voices

"It think how all things have developed is extraordinary, especially technology."

"A risk I took for no good reason was doing a snowboarding jump or going fast, just to show off. I could have gotten hurt, and my parents would have been mad."

" If you look closely at everything, you will be grateful because life is truly miraculous."

"I love the outdoor chapel at my camp. There is something special about going to the same place every day for services. And it is outdoors and beautiful."

" I think that everything we do, everything we see, and everything we hear is amazing on a certain level. If you define 'amazing' as things that are hard to explain or simply unnecessarily beautiful, many things, most things, even all things are amazing. I define amazing as extraordinary, incredible things, such as someone surviving a bad car crash, a firefighter saving a life, or the Red Sea splitting open."

"Judaism has influenced my political views. I'm socially very liberal, and my Reform Jewish values have taught me the importance of accepting people's differences."

" I love playing baseball. Something about it speaks to me. The motion, stimulation, physical exertion, and competition combine to make the perfect game. It's also a great way to make friends with people from other towns. The whole thing kind of captures the wonder of life."

"I love playing guitar. I am good at it, and it can lead to big life moments and opportunity. It makes me feel better than anything."

"When I play a sport, I always wear a mezuzah around my neck. It makes me feel that something is protecting me."

"Every Sunday I help special needs kids play sports. The first year it was for my mitzvah project for my bar mitzvah, but later it became something more. I have my own buddy I am personally with every time. His parents run the entire thing, and they told me that I have made a significant different in my buddy's life. When they said that, it made me not want to take things for granted."

"We have Jewish values—tzedakah, tikkun olam. But we are normal teens, we hang out with friends, we go to school, do our homework."

"I think that God works in ways we don't understand, and we will always be guessing where God is, who God is, and what God does. But that's the point of religion: the unknown."

Did You Know?

- According to the National Aeronautics and Space Administration (NASA), about 70 percent of the human body is made up of water, and more than 70 percent of Earth is covered in water, too. What a wondrous coincidence.

- In the international space program, twelve of the astronauts have been Jews. Ten of these amazing explorers and scientists came from the United States, one from Israel, and one from the former Soviet Union. Jewish spaceflight got off to an inauspicious start in 1964 when Soviet cosmonaut Boris Volynov was prohibited from participating in the mission because of his Jewish lineage. Not buckling under pressure, five years later he became the first Jewish person in space when he commanded the Soyuz 5 mission in 1969.

- While Jews make up only 0.18 percent of the world's population, roughly 20 percent of Nobel Prize winners—both men and women—are Jews. These award winners reflect the emphasis Judaism places on education, wonder, and discovery. We can stand in amazement at the excellence of these individuals.

Get Yourself a Teacher

The Maccabeats

The Wonder of Music

Ten million YouTube viewers couldn't be wrong. The Macca-beats all-male a cappella group started by students at Yeshiva University entertains young and old with songs that convey their love of Jewish life. The Maccabeats have lifted audience spirits at concerts in JCCs, synagogues, jazz clubs, conventions, theaters, and more across five continents and over thirty states and provinces. They've even performed at the White House at a reception hosted by President Barack Obama for Jewish community leaders from across the country in honor of Jewish American Heritage Month. But most important, these guys take contemporary songs and Jewish music and infuse them with their own spirituality and love of life.

Mendy Pellin

The Wonder of Laughter

There is nothing better for the soul than a good belly laugh. Mendy Pellin is a Hasidic comic who has even appeared in the movie *Moneyball* with Brad Pitt. Blending Hasidic wisdom with unexpected humor, Pellin overcomes stereotypes often associated with ultra-Orthodox Jews. His entertaining Web-based news show, *The Mendy Report*, attracts over fifty thousand viewers per broadcast. Contrary to popular belief, being a very observant Jew does not mean you can't have fun. Pellin shows that savoring humor and joy in life is truly heavenly. Pellin represents the idea that the Divine can also be found in laughter.

Steven Spielberg

The Wonder of Movies

Steven Spielberg is one of the most creative, powerful, and successful moviemakers in Hollywood. His films amaze us, inspire us, make us laugh and cry, bring us joy, and bring history to life. Spielberg made his first movie at age sixteen. It was a science-fiction thriller that he wrote, produced, and starred in. His dad rented a local movie theater so he could share his film with the public. That event launched him on a path that has been truly incredible. Perhaps his most impactful Jewish film is *Schindler's List*, a story of the Holocaust. This movie is testimony before all humankind about the events of the Holocaust. It also teaches how sacred life is.

Learn

The Rules of Checkers

The following story tells us that games, like checkers, can teach us valuable lessons about life. Let's look at the rules of checkers that Rabbi Nahum explained and see what they can tell us about being alive:

> It is told that Rabbi Nahum, a son of the Rizhyner rabbi, once visited the study house unannounced on one of the days of Hanukkah. He found the students playing checkers, as was the custom in those days. When they saw the *tzaddik* [righteous teacher] appear in the room, they became bewildered and speechless. The *tzaddik*, however,

gave a friendly nod and asked, "Do you know the rules of checkers?" The students were intimidated and remained silent. So he gave the answer himself: "I will tell you the rules of checkers. The first is that you may only make one move at a time. The second, you may only move forward and never back. And the third, when you have reached the end, you may move wherever you want."[2]

⯟ What do you think the first two rules—you can only make one move at a time, and you can't go backward—mean? What does this teach you? Do you agree with these ideas?

⯟ Describe a time when it would have been helpful to remember these rules in your life.

⯟ What do you think the last rule—when you get to the end, you can move anywhere you want—means?

Rules for Living Wisely

Go, eat your bread in gladness, and drink your wine in joy; for your action was long ago approved by God. Let your clothes always be freshly washed.... Enjoy happiness with someone you love all the fleeting days of life that have been granted to you under the sun—all your fleeting days. For that alone is what you can get out of life.... Whatever it is in your power to do, do with all your might.

(Ecclesiastes 9:7–10)

The book of Ecclesiastes (or *Kohelet* in Hebrew) offers some rules for living and reminds us we should enjoy life. Judaism is not a religion of pain or self-denial. It should be a religion of joy. *Kohelet* tells us to eat and drink well, enjoy the company of people you love, and do what is in your power to do. *Kohelet* does not promise a heavenly reward or say the world will be fair; it says that we should enjoy and get the most out of our "fleeting days."

- ✡ Do you agree with *Kohelet*'s approach to life? Why or why not?
- ✡ Is *Kohelet*'s recipe for living satisfactory? Judaism believes in doing more than just surviving. How does *tikkun olam*, or repairing and transforming the world, fit in?
- ✡ What do you think *Kohelet* means by stating, "Your action was long ago approved by God"?

Omnipresent God

The Infinite One exists in everything. Do not say, "This is a stone and not God." God forbid! Rather, all existence is God, and the stone is a thing filled by divinity.

(Moses Cordovero, *Shiur Komah* 206b)[3]

- ✡ This teaching tells us that everything, even a stone, is a part of God. We don't worship stones, but we can see them as a piece of something bigger. Here, Cordovero's words are reminding us that when we use words like "King" to refer to God, God is not really a King but an indescribable Infinity that fills and surrounds the universe. You can see God in nature or everyday objects. Does this kind of understanding of God speak to you? Why or why not?

⭐ Replace the word "stone" in this teaching with some object in your home, such as a computer, glass of water, soccer ball, or musical instrument. Does this change how you look at the world?

⭐ Choose an ordinary object in the room. Explain why it is amazing when you stop and think about it.

Counting Your Blessings

When you hear the rooster crow [in the morning], you should say: "Blessed is the One who gives the rooster the understanding to distinguish between day and night." When you open your eyes, you should say: "Blessed is the One who opens the eyes of the blind." When you stretch yourself and sit up, you should say: "Blessed is the One who frees the captive." When you dress, you should say: "Blessed is the One who clothes the naked." When you stand up, you should say: "Blessed is the One who straightens those who are bowed down." When you step on to the ground, you should say: "Blessed is the One who spreads the earth on the waters." When you begin to walk, you should say: "Blessed is the One who makes firm each person's steps." When you tie your shoes, you should say: "Blessed is the One who has given me all that I need." When you tie your belt, you should say: "Blessed is the One who girds Israel with strength." When you cover your head, you should say: "Blessed is the One who crowns Israel with glory."... When you wash your face, you should say: "Blessed is the One who has removed sleep from my eyes and slumber from my eyelids."

(Talmud, *B'rachot* 60b)

> Rabbi Meir used to say: A person is obligated to say one
> hundred blessings a day.
>
> **(Talmud, *M'nachot* 43b)**

A *b'rachah* (blessing) asks us to pay attention to something.
Each one of the morning blessings is said along with a different
action a person does in the morning. The act of opening your
eyes in the morning goes with a blessing for "opening the eyes
of the blind," and so on.

- Why should we pay attention to these everyday actions?
- What might blessings remind us of as we go through
  our daily routine?
- What kind of life would we live if we tried to live
  by Rabbi Meir's rule of aspiring to say one hundred
  blessings a day?
- Do you think trying to say a hundred blessings each
  day would interfere with other things you want to do,
  or would it make life more meaningful?
- Some believe a blessing only "counts" if someone says
  "Amen" after you say it. How does this complicate
  things? Why do you think some believe this is a
  requirement?
- If you were to write your own blessing for something
  that happens to you each day, what would it be?

What Do I Think?

Name some special times you have felt "radical amazement."

_____

_____

_____

_____

_____

_____

_____

_____

_____

_____

What makes you feel most alive? Why?

_____

_____

_____

_____

If ordinary things are actually amazing, why do people get bored? What can you do about it when you feel that way?

_____

_____

_____

_____

_____

_____

When have you felt that you belonged to
something bigger than yourself? Where were you?

_____

_____

_____

_____

_____

_____

_____

_____

_____

_____

_____

Capture any of your additional thoughts or questions here.

_____

_____

_____

_____

_____

_____

_____

_____

Text Connection

מָה־רַבּוּ מַעֲשֶׂיךָ יְיָ כֻּלָּם בְּחָכְמָה
עָשִׂיתָ מָלְאָה הָאָרֶץ קִנְיָנֶךָ

*Mah rabu ma'asecha Adonai! Kulam b'chochmah
asita; mal'ah ha'aretz kinyanecha.*

Adonai, You have made so much! In
wisdom You have made them all; the
Earth is full of Your creations.

—Psalm 104:24

Enough already

Why am I so stressed out?

וַיְכַל אֱלֹהִים בַּיּוֹם
הַשְּׁבִיעִי מְלַאכְתּוֹ אֲשֶׁר עָשָׂה

***Vay'chal Elohim bayom
hash'vi'i m'lachto asher asah.***

God ceased work on
the seventh day.
—Genesis 2:2

Enough Already

Why am I so stressed out?

"So what do you like to do?"

You may be surprised to learn that as a rabbi, I spend a great deal, if not most, of my professional time with twelve- to sixteen-year-olds. Preparing students for bar and bat mitzvah, teaching tenth grade in Hebrew school, and hanging out with our youth group have let me keep in touch with something of my "inner teenager." I take notes on each kid: who likes to play guitar, who likes to play "basketball-baseball-soccer" (kids who play one usually play them all), and who is in the school play. But almost always, the first answer to "So what do you like to do?" is "Hang out with my friends."

"Hanging-out time" has rapidly shrunk since I was a teenager. As a teenager today, you have so many more opportunities than I had. A teenage guy today can easily go from playing basketball to singing in a rock band to traveling to Washington, DC, for a youth simulation of the United Nations ... to anything. Every day is packed.

On top of all these activities, the amount of homework seems to have grown. "How many hours of homework do you have?" I sometimes ask. "About three." When I ask if that is normal for a school night, the answer is always "yes." That doesn't leave much time for sleep, does it?

Something else has changed radically in just one generation. You not only have a packed schedule inside and outside of school, you—along with everyone else—now carry around a device that allows you to stay in constant touch with your friends, to check on someone's status, to send someone a picture, or to send a link to something you found funny or interesting. While doing your homework, you can also chat and listen to music and watch TV. While reading a book, you often also have a video going on off to the side. While playing a video game, you talk to someone else. You are the first generation of people I would call "radical multitaskers." You do everything at once. And many of you are incredibly stressed out with all this activity and connection. The words "hanging out with my friends" come with a certain kind of longing, because that time has become rare.

Your generation lives in a new world. In the time of your grandparents, people tended to work from nine to five. They were home at six for a home-cooked meal prepared by your grandmother, who was home a lot of the day. When she called the family to dinner, they sat together with no TV or cell phones. One or two generations ago, people were likely to know their neighbors, and all the kids on the block would form spontaneous teams for pickup games.

The generations of your parents and grandparents jumped full force into e-mail, mobile phones, and working all the time. The workweek has expanded, so that people leave for work earlier and come home later. And people need to constantly check their phones, being available to work and be productive 24/7. Men in particular often have their self-esteem and identity caught up in their work. They cannot seem to stop looking at the little screen on their hip or kept in their pocket.

In our radical multitasking world, contemporary culture pushes you to do all that was previously done and more. If life were a multiple-choice test, today's answer to every question would be (d) "all of the above."

Your amazing ability to do everything at once all the time comes with many costs. One is your ability to give undivided attention to something important. The times when you get to just concentrate and appreciate something you love to do is getting squeezed. When was the last time you had all day to do nothing but something that you wanted, free from what others expect?

People need your undivided attention and many have a hard time giving it or getting it. True friendship or love demands that you listen to other people with everything that you have. It means looking at them in the face to hear not only what they are saying but to see what they are not saying. Relationships are sacred, and they deserve not to be multitasked or done virtually.

We need more hanging-out, real time. Quality time. One winter when I was a teenager, I spent the night sleeping over my friend's house. After a great day playing video games, having a snowball fight, and exploring the woods behind his house, I crawled into a sleeping bag on his floor. I was a little surprised when my friend's dad came down to talk with us before we went to sleep. My friend and I began talking about all the things we were going to do the next day, when his father said, "Remember that you can do *anything* that you want to do, but you can't do *everything* you want to do."

Two thousand years ago, Judaism created a relief from radical multitasking and the stress that comes with it. That relief is called Shabbat and it's one of Judaism's great gifts to the world. Traditionally, Shabbat involves going to synagogue and having special meals, but it does not need to be understood only as a strictly religious day. The deeper message of Shabbat is to take time to stop doing what we usually do and instead spend time alone or with others. We need a little Shabbat break not just once a week but every day. You are allowed to say, "Enough already."

Shabbat means putting the mobile phone down and looking into the face of the person sitting next to you. It means not doing everything at once but doing one thing with pleasure and happiness. It means having time to talk to people without interruption. Shabbat means that in order to connect, you have to first disconnect. You then create space in your life for a walk, for a conversation, and for yourself.

We all know that we need quiet time, but nevertheless it takes a great act of willpower to stop multitasking. Shabbat moments require personal strength and restraint. Sometimes you have to just pretend for a moment that something is all done to give yourself the freedom to take a break. But hanging-out time, otherwise known as time for relationships with others, nature, and your soul, is part of creation. Even God needed to stop after six days and rest on the seventh. You deserve nothing less.
—**RABBI JOSEPH**

Find Yourself a Friend: Teen Voices

"One time, I decided not to do my math homework for no reason at all. I just thought, you know what, YOLO!! [you only live once]."

"Life would be less stressful if grades didn't matter."

"My parents acknowledge all of my stresses, so they know they are there. The thing is, they don't understand the magnitude or importance of some stresses."

"My parents do not understand why I am aggravated at 8:00 p.m. after waking up at 5:50 a.m., having school, doing homework, having extracurricular activities until 7:00, and then watching my little sister."

"When I get home, I have ice cream or something, or a snack. Lately, I've been taking a nap. And my parents send me too many texts from work. I wish they would just text, 'Hope your day was good,' instead of asking how my day was."

"Soccer sometimes is too intense. We have late-night practices, and I get leg cramps."

"I've already taken myself out of contention for Yale! I got a B in Spanish, so that is over!"

"I love soccer, basketball, my band, video games, watching TV, and my Jewish youth group. I love things where I get to hang out with my friends and do things I am good at."

"I think I do a perfect amount of activities ... but my mom begs to differ."

"We do not really celebrate Shabbat often, but when we do, we do it as a family."

" My favorite activity is going to
dances with our regional youth group
because of all the people I get to
meet and the fun I get to have."

"To relax, I listen to soothing music to
calm down when I am stressed out."

Did You Know?

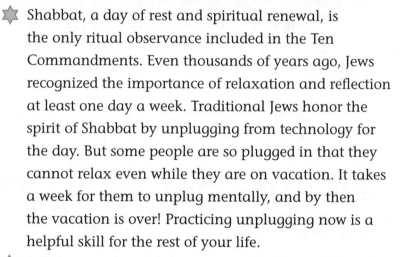

🔯 Shabbat, a day of rest and spiritual renewal, is
the only ritual observance included in the Ten
Commandments. Even thousands of years ago, Jews
recognized the importance of relaxation and reflection
at least one day a week. Traditional Jews honor the
spirit of Shabbat by unplugging from technology for
the day. But some people are so plugged in that they
cannot relax even while they are on vacation. It takes
a week for them to unplug mentally, and by then
the vacation is over! Practicing unplugging now is a
helpful skill for the rest of your life.

🔯 A little stress is good, but too much stress negatively
affects your mind and your body. Headaches, muscle
tension, chest pain, fatigue, sleep problems, and upset
stomach are just some of the many ways stress shows
up in our lives, as cited by the American Psychological
Association's "Stress in America" report.[1] Stress might
have something to do with obesity, because we try to
satisfy our desire for something soothing by eating.

⯩ One side of stress is worry about your body and accepting who you are physically. Most of the time, people think of girls when they think of caring about how you and your body look, but guys of course care about that, too. Am I too short? Too heavy? Too skinny? Too muscular? How do I smell? What does an ideal man look like? Can I really look like that? Part of being at peace with yourself is not to buy in to advertising stereotypes. You need to take care of your body to be healthy and have good hygiene, but very few guys look like Hollywood stars.

⯩ The film *Race to Nowhere* exposes American high school students' pressure to succeed. Shown in more than five thousand schools, universities, theaters, hospitals, corporations, and community centers, this film has sparked serious conversations on stress reduction in the educational system. Is there something you can do to unclutter your life?

Get Yourself a Teacher

Rabbi Moshe Waldoks

Time for Meditation

For ten years, Rabbi Moshe Waldoks recognized the need for a Jewish meditation center to help people cultivate better physical and emotional health and well-being within a Jewish context. In 2005, his vision was realized when Nishmat Hayyim, "Breath of Life," started its first programs in Massachusetts. On the organization's website, one of the teachers defines Jewish meditation this way: "Our aim is to support Jewish spiritual life; to provide accessible gateways into Judaism; and to cultivate better physical and emotional health and well-being in a Jewish context."[2] Meditation provides relief from the hectic demands of living in this multitasking age. It helps people slow down, get centered, and find the strength and calm to de-stress. Meditation also has the potential to connect people to Jewish spirituality and wisdom. Can you envision yourself meditating?

Tamir Goodman

Time for Shabbat ... and Basketball

Sports Illustrated dubbed Tamir Goodman the "Jewish Jordan" when he was a high-school basketball player averaging more than thirty-five points per game.[3] Tamir received a scholarship to play basketball at the University of Maryland, one of the top-ranked basketball teams in the country. Tamir declined the offer. As an Orthodox Jew, he chose not to practice and play games on Friday nights and Saturdays. After a short time playing for another university in Maryland, Tamir fulfilled a dream to move to Israel and play professional basketball there. As he explains,

> Some people may have the opinion that Judaism restricts you or prevents you from fulfilling your dreams, but it's really the opposite. The Torah and Judaism empower us, give us guidance, motivation, inspiration, tell us what our intentions should be, and they're the blueprint for life and whatever we're doing.

What do you think of Tamir's point of view?

Matisyahu

Time for Music

Matisyahu is the Hebrew name and stage name of the American musician Matthew Paul Miller. Known for blending traditional Jewish themes with reggae, rock, hip-hop, and beatboxing, his creative music contains Jewish heroes like the Baal Shem Tov, prayers in Hebrew, and stories of Israel—along with universal inspiration found in Judaism. One way to chill and relax is by listening to music. As Matisyahu says himself, "Music taps into a very deep place and speaks to us in a way that regular words can't."[4] What music do you like? How does this music make you feel?

Learn

Working to Live or Living to Work?

> The Six Days are the beginning, in which everything was created. Shabbat is the end and ultimate purpose.... They are points that form a circle around an inner point, which is Shabbat.
>
> **(Rabbi Nachman of Breslov, *Likutei Moharan* 2:39)**

Normally we think of a week beginning with day one and then progressing in a line to the seventh day. If we stop on the weekend, our purpose is to rest so that we can then get back to work. In this short passage, Rabbi Nachman teaches two important lessons. First, he is teaching that the six days of work exist for the sake of the seventh, not the other way around. In other words, we work to live; we do not live in order to work.

Second, we don't have to think of the week in a straight line. Another way to think about the week is to put Shabbat in the center of a wheel with six spokes sticking out. The days of work revolve around an inner point—Shabbat revitalization. Every day draws energy from Shabbat.

- ✡ Do you find yourself thinking of work, chores, and homework during times when you should be relaxing, being with friends, or on vacation? When did this start? Does it bother you?
- ✡ When are you most stressed out?
- ✡ What do you think a good balance between living and working would look like?
- ✡ According to this teaching, Shabbat is not just about one day out of seven but about energy in each day. When during the day can you stop and take a "Shabbat moment"?

Disconnect in Order to Connect

Six days a week we seek to dominate the world; on the seventh day we try to dominate the self ... to set apart one day a week for freedom, a day on which we would not use the instruments which have been so easily turned into weapons of destruction, a day for being with ourselves, a day of detachment from the vulgar, of independence of external obligations, a day on which we stop worshiping the idols of technical civilization.[5]

(Abraham Joshua Heschel, *The Sabbath*)

- ✡ Do you think it is realistic to "set apart one day a week for freedom"? Why or why not?

⭐ What do you think Heschel means when he writes that we try to dominate the world, but during Shabbat we try to dominate the self?

⭐ What are some of the best things about computers and mobile phones? What are some of the drawbacks? How do they make life easier? How do they increase stress? What do you think Heschel means when he refers to "instruments which have been so easily turned into weapons of destruction"? What is being destroyed?

⭐ If you could have an hour each day without chores, errands, or homework and could do anything, what would you do? Who would you do it with?

Hey Moses! Stop, Look, and Listen!

When God chooses Moses to be the leader of the Jewish people, God starts with a kind of test. God presents Moses with a burning bush that does not turn to ashes:

> An angel of *Adonai* appeared to him in a blazing fire out of a bush. He gazed, and there was a bush all aflame, yet the bush was not consumed. Moses said, "I must turn aside to look at this marvelous sight; why doesn't the bush burn up?" When *Adonai* saw that he had turned aside to look, God called to him.
>
> (Exodus 3:2–4)

⭐ The Torah says, "When *Adonai* saw that he had turned aside to look...." Focusing on these words, what was the test God had devised for Moses?

✡ How long do you think it would have taken Moses to notice that the bush was not burning up? Would he have gotten it immediately, or would it have taken some time to figure this out?

✡ If Moses had been listening to music, texting, and riding by in his SUV, do you think Moses would have noticed the burning bush? Why or why not? What might this say about us and our lives?

✡ In this episode, the Torah teaches that learning to stop and pay attention is a primary spiritual step. Do you agree? Why or why not?

✡ Can you think of an occasion when you had time to stop and notice something that you otherwise might have missed?

What Do I Think?

Do you think you do too many activities? Too little? Why or why not?

_____

_____

_____

_____

_____

_____

_____

What do you do to relax?

Name one thing you wish you could change to reduce stress in your life.

_____

_____

_____

_____

_____

What does Shabbat mean to you? To your family?

_____

_____

_____

_____

_____

_____

_____

Capture any of your additional thoughts or questions here.

_____

_____

_____

_____

_____

_____

_____

_____

_____

_____

Text Connection

וַיְכַל אֱלֹהִים בַּיּוֹם
הַשְּׁבִיעִי מְלַאכְתּוֹ אֲשֶׁר עָשָׂה

Vay'chal Elohim bayom hash'vi'i m'lachto asher asah.

God ceased work on the seventh day.

—Genesis 2:2

"Before I went to sleepaway camp, my dad gave me like a three-hour talk about the birds and the bees. I was stuck with him in the car during the drive for the whole time."

"Before I went to sleepaway camp, my dad gave me like a three-hour talk about the birds and the bees. I was stuck with him in the car during the drive for the whole time."

"I think it's really bad that everyone is getting into sex and stuff at a much earlier age than back in the day—most people aren't quite ready for it when they find themselves in a situation."

Falling in lust, falling in love

I can't help thinking about sex, but I don't know what's right for me.

קְדֹשִׁים תִּהְיוּ

K'doshim tih'yu.

You shall be holy.
—Leviticus 19:2

"Kids call each other 'fag' or say, 'That is so gay' because they're insecure about themselves and/or their sexuality."

"My parents think that every girl I'm friends with is my girlfriend."

Falling in Lust, Falling in Love

I can't help thinking about sex, but I don't know what's right for me.

"I do not want to go to college being a virgin."

"We can have sex, but tell me you love me first."

"It's okay to have sex if you both don't have feelings for each other. Then it's just fooling around and no one gets hurt."

"Oral sex isn't really sex."

These are just a few of the things you may hear as a teenager. But this does not prevent guys from thinking and joking about it all the time. Some of the talk comes about because boys want to show other boys how advanced they are. Everything in our environment plays into this attitude. For example, clothes are designed to make us look sexy. Our media uses sex to sell everything—from cars to medicine. And it's not just the ads. Popular television shows have become hypersexualized.

It is difficult not to think about sex as a teenage guy. While there is a great deal of sex education available in the world, guys still carry around a lot of confusion and anxiety when it comes to sex.

Even the most strictly religiously observant Jews struggle with living out a healthy sex ethic. In college, at Hillel, there was a joke that some of the guys must belong to the "612 club." That is, they observed all 613 commandments except the one that said they couldn't have sex. On the other hand, some young

Orthodox Jews practiced being *shomer n'giah*, which means that unmarried girls and boys who are not close relatives should not touch each other at all. Conservative, Reform, and other forms of Judaism do not follow these laws.

As with all physical needs, like eating and drinking, Judaism values the good in sex but also believes that sex needs parameters or limits. Denying or repressing our physical impulses is wrong sometimes but appropriate at others. For example, the Torah specifies all the sexual relations that Jews must not have, such as incest. Learning to control one's sexual desires is part of becoming a civilized human being. Judaism seeks to sanctify the human animal, to take a natural act and elevate it to something holy.

This chapter is not about sex education. It is about some of the values that should go into making healthy, smart choices about sex grounded in Judaism, values such as the following:

> *Emet* / אֱמֶת: honesty
>
> *B'riyut* / בְּרִיאוּת: health
>
> *Mishpat* / מִשְׁפָּט: fairness
>
> *Mishpachah* / מִשְׁפָּחָה: family
>
> *Tz'niyut* / צְנִיעוּת: modesty and privacy
>
> *B'rit* / בְּרִית: covenantal relationship
>
> *Simchah* / שִׂמְחָה: joy
>
> *Ahavah* / אַהֲבָה: love (including self-esteem, caring, support, and empathy)
>
> *K'dushah* / קְדוּשָׁה: holiness, to be exclusively set apart for a higher purpose.[1]

In this view, Judaism does not condemn sex as something dirty, wrong, or sinful. Lifelong celibacy is not a Jewish value. There are no Jewish monks or nuns. In fact, the first words God spoke to Adam in the book of Genesis was to encourage him to have many children. Rabbis are expected to have families. The Jewish marriage agreement known as the *ketubah* alludes to conjugal rights where married partners are supposed to have sex with each other. There is even a small ancient Jewish book on the holiness of sex called "The Holy Letter" (*Iggeret HaKodesh*):

> Know that the sexual intercourse of man with his wife is holy and pure when done properly, in the proper time and with the proper intention. No one should think that sexual intercourse is ugly and loathsome, God forbid!
> (*Iggeret HaKodesh*)

Certainly, this text makes clear that sex within a loving marriage is something to be celebrated. We should note that all discussions about sex in Jewish texts concern heterosexual relations. The earliest Rabbis even wrote into Jewish law how often a man should have sex with his wife:

> The obligation as it is understood in the Torah is that for idle men, every day. For workers, twice a week. For donkey drivers [who travel during the week transporting goods but are home on the weekends], once a week. For camel drivers [who are gone for longer stretches of time], once a month. For sailors, once every six months.
> (*Mishnah K'tubot 5:6*)

As awkward as it may be to talk about sex, there are also serious reasons not to have sex. The important idea to remember is that sex has consequences. Sex should be preceded and accompanied by thinking. Teenage guys may not be ready to think things through in the heat of the moment, such as always making sure sex is consensual and always using condoms. The only foolproof way to avoid disease and pregnancy is abstinence.

Jewish values should inform our behavior and choices when it comes to sex, but in the twenty-first century, it is a challenge to remember these values when sexualized material and behavior are everywhere. Consider just some contemporary challenges to Jewish values that the average teen guy confronts:

- Pornography: With access to the Internet on any mobile device or computer, pornography is available as never before. Pornography capitalizes on curiosity, excitement, and fantasy, but how does it accord with the Jewish values of modesty, relationship, and love? What happens when sex is not an act of sacred intimacy but a commodity to be graphically exploited? Or a momentary thrill?

- Sexual fads: Generations of teenagers have been hooking up (or trying to). But kids having oral sex or more at a young age may not be thinking about sexually transmitted diseases (STDs) or how this affects someone's reputation. Sexual behavior at younger ages has even been happening at bar and bat mitzvah parties.[2] An experience that lasts a few minutes can have lifelong consequences. What do you think of kids doing this at age thirteen? What do you think of girls who give sex this way? Is there a double standard for girls as opposed to guys?

- Often people assume that heterosexuality is universal. But the truth is that many of our family members and friends may be gay, lesbian, or bisexual (people attracted to members of both sexes). Teens don't usually know who they are sexually and are trying to figure things out for themselves. We now know that being gay is not a lifestyle choice or a preference. It is part of a person's basic physical and emotional identity. Yet Jewish law has in no uncertain terms condemned homosexual activity, with statements such as "Do not lie with a male as one lies with a woman; it is an abhorrence" (Leviticus 18:22). Regardless, some Jewish guys know they are gay and are attracted to other guys. Some streams of Judaism have decided to be open to gays and lesbians on the basis of the idea that God made each one of us in the divine image. If God made me this way, how can my sexual identity be wrong? How accepting are we of other people's identity, as a Jewish community? And how accepting are you personally? Even if we say we are open and inclusive, how often do you hear the phrase "That's so gay" or "You're a fag"?

✡ A frequently ignored aspect of sexuality is transgendered identity. This term refers to the fact that some children who are born with male genitals strongly believe that they are girls, and some with female genitals believe they are boys. Children's and adult's sexual attributes can be changed with surgery. Jewish communities have not dealt extensively with the issue of people with transgendered histories. One contemporary artist, Israeli-born Yishay Garbasz, was born a boy but always knew she was a girl. Not a girlie girl, but a girl nonetheless. Yishay has created several pieces of art that explore her identity. For example, Yishay has created an artist's book composed of daily photographs of her naked body for a year before her corrective (gender alignment) surgery and daily for one year after. She wants to document the entire process so that people will understand how much effort it took to bring her body in line with her feelings and identity.

Many of the issues related to sex ultimately deal with respect. Do you respect others? Do you respect yourself? Do you respect girls in general? And do you respect girls who "sleep around"? It is easy to confuse love and lust. The choice of a moment can have lasting consequences. How we behave and the choices we make define who we are.
—RABBI JOSEPH and DR. SHULA

Find Yourself a Friend: Teen Voices

" I feel pressured (by my friends who are having sex) to have sex with my girlfriend. I'm not sure if I'm ready."

"A lot of my friends make jokes about sex and different types of positions/moves. I think that sex and hooking up isn't taken as seriously as they should be."

" What happens if I injure her while having sex?"

"I feel like kids our age watch a lot of porn, which gives us a false sense of knowing what we're doing."

" I don't want to get anyone pregnant. That scares the crap out of me."

"I think it's really bad that everyone is getting into sex and stuff at a much earlier age than back in the day—most people aren't quite ready for it when they find themselves in a situation."

"Kids call each other 'fag' or say, 'That is so gay' because they're insecure about themselves and/or their sexuality."

"Before I went to sleepaway camp, my dad gave me like a three-hour talk about the birds and the bees. I was stuck with him in car during the drive for the whole time."

"One day I was playing basketball with two of my friends. Earlier that day I had told one of them about a girl I had a crush on. When the topic of girls came up during our game, my friend slipped and accidentally told the others who I liked. I was really pissed that he shared what was then my biggest secret."

"My parents think that every girl I'm friends with is my girlfriend."

Did You Know?

As reported in an article in the *Jewish Daily Forward*,[3] Camp Tawonga, a Jewish camp in San Francisco, has a HAKWACO policy, an acronym for "hugging and kissing with all clothes on." This means that it is okay to hug and kiss as long as no clothes come off. Of course, where there are rules, there are also ways of getting around them. "We don't want campers to feel sexual behavior is bad, but we want them to focus on friendship and community at camp," said director Jamie Simon-Harris. When teen boys and girls are together at camp, it is probably impossible to keep them apart sexually, but camp directors try their best. The 1997 comedy film *Camp Stories*, starring Elliott Gould and Jerry Stiller, offers a wonderful take on the administration's attempt to repress sexuality at camp. The 2001 film *Wet Hot American Summer* forever branded Jewish sleepaway camps as hookup central. But also, guess what? Camp Tawonga also has a *chuppah* (wedding canopy) signed by married couples who met years before at camp.

⭐ Back when your great-great-grandparents wanted to get married, and even today in some parts of the Jewish world, people consulted matchmakers to introduce them to potential spouses. Today, many Jewish single adults turn to JDate, a popular online dating site, to meet Jewish singles. Other websites include JWed, JMom.com, JSingles, JMatch, and Saw You at Sinai.com.

⭐ The kiss, a universal image of love and affection, is a popular subject in paintings and photographs, including "The Birthday Kiss" by the famous Jewish Russian artist Marc Chagall (1887–1985).

Get Yourself a Teacher

Frat Brother

Thinking "She" Could Be His Sister

At a fraternity house at a university in North Carolina, one of the most popular events to attract freshman pledges was to have girls from a sorority dress in bikinis and welcome guys to the house. This understandably attracted a lot of people. The guys would stare and talk about the girls. However, one year a fraternity brother hesitated and asked himself, "What if one of those girls was my sister?" He shared his mixed feelings with his fraternity brothers, and they decided to stop hosting the event. Do you think these girls were being exploited? Why or why not?

Rabbi Adin Steinsaltz

Thinking Sex Should Be Holy

Time magazine calls Rabbi Adin Steinsaltz "a once-in-a-millennium-scholar."[4] This prominent Israeli rabbi offered his view of the importance of sex to the Aleph Society, a group of his supporters, on their 2012 Global Day of Jewish Learning:

> Judaism does not view sex as unclean, as a necessary humiliation for the purposes of increase. Judaism does not see sexuality only as an instrument for the propagation of the human race, a means of being fruitful and multiplying. According to Jewish tradition, in the right context and when engaged with conscious purpose, sex is seen as a positive commandment because,

in contrast to food and money, sexual pleasure is not connected with ownership. It is a pleasure derived from giving and being connected with another; it can become a most meaningful expression of love, charity and benevolence. It can become an expression of holiness.[5]

Israeli Author Amos Oz

Thinking about Why His Grandfather Was a Chick Magnet

In his autobiographical novel *Tale of Love and Darkness*, Amos Oz shares his grandfather's secrets to success with women: he was a good listener, he had genuine interest in what he heard, he was empathetic, and he loved women and sex. Here are excerpts from the book that illustrate the bond Oz's grandfather had with women:

> Before he had managed to wipe the dust of Grandma's burial off his shoes, Grandpa's home was full of women offering condolences, encouragement, freedom from loneliness, sympathy. They never left him alone, nourishing him with hot meals, comforting him with apple cake, and he apparently enjoyed not letting them leave him alone. He was always attracted to women—all women, both the beautiful ones and those whose beauty other men were incapable of seeing.... He sat for hours at his table on the discreet upstairs floor of Café Atara in Ben Yehuda Street, dressed in a navy blue suit, with a polka-dot tie ... always surrounded by a bevy of well-preserved women in their fifties or sixties.... What was the secret of Grandpa's charm?... He possessed a quality

that is hardly ever found among men, a marvelous quality that for many women is the sexiest in a man: He listened. He did not just politely pretend to listen, while impatiently waiting for her to finish what she was saying and shut up. He did not break his partner's sentence and finish it for her. He did not cut in to sum up what she was saying so as to move on to another subject. He did not let his interlocutress talk into thin air while he prepared in his head the reply he would make when she finally finished. He did not pretend to be interested or entertained, he really was…. *Nu*, what: they talked and talked to him to their heart's content, even about the most private, secret, vulnerable things, while he sat and listened, wisely, gently, with empathy and patience. Or rather with pleasure and feeling. There are many men around who love sex but hate women. My grandfather, I believe, loved both.[6]

Learn

What Is the Story of the Snake and the Fruit Really About?

God commanded Adam [and through Adam, also Eve], saying, "Of every tree of the garden you are free to eat; but as for the Tree of Knowledge, you must not to eat of it; for as soon as you eat of it, you shall die…. But the serpent was the most seductive of all of the animals. He said to the woman, "Did God really say: You shall not eat of the fruit of any tree of the garden?... You won't die. Your eyes will be opened.".... When the woman saw that the tree was good for eating and a delight to the eyes, and that the tree was also desirable as a source of wisdom, she took of its fruit and ate. She also gave some to her husband, and he ate. The eyes of both of them were opened, and they knew that they were naked.

(Genesis 2:16–17, 3:1, 3:4–7)

It is possible to read this famous story about Adam and Eve in many ways. God tells Adam not to eat fruit from the Tree of Knowledge. However, a snake convinces Eve to eat of the fruit, and then she and Adam are changed forever. One interpretation is that the story is about sexual awareness, that the "Knowledge" is carnal knowledge or sexual experience. The snake and the fruit are symbolic of the sexual act. By having sex, Adam and Eve lose their childhood innocence and become self-conscious.

- In this story, sex and knowledge are closely linked. In the Hebrew Bible, Adam "knowing" Eve is a euphemism for sex. Sex is intended to be an act of intimacy, to "know in the biblical sense." Why does intimacy make sex special? What do you think happens if there is sex without intimacy, without really knowing someone?
- This story is also about "firsts." You only get one first. What changes in Adam and Eve after this first sexual act? What might that mean for us?
- God tells Adam not to rush ahead and eat the fruit, but the snake says to go for it. What are the pressures today to have sex sooner rather than later? What are some good reasons to wait?

Where Did Adam and Eve Have Sex?

Returning to Adam and Eve, the Torah relates that they were naked together in the Garden of Eden. Adam and Eve had sex, and Eve gave birth to a son:

> They were both naked, the man and his wife, and were not ashamed.... The man knew Eve his wife, and she became pregnant and bore Cain....
>
> **(Genesis 2:25, 4:1)**

A biblical commentator named Rashi (Rabbi Shlomo ben Yitzchak, tenth century, France) points out a small but significant detail:

> "The man knew" should be understood as "had known" already before Adam sinned and was driven out of Eden. The act of sex, conception, and birth of Cain took place before any sin [while they were still in the Garden of Eden].
>
> **(Rashi on Genesis 4:1)**

Rashi shows that they had sex while still in the Garden of Eden and not after they were expelled. He did this because in his time and place, the specific Christian culture in which he lived thought sex was dirty and sinful. The Christian ideal was to be a virgin and to be chaste. But Rashi is pointing out that, according to the Hebrew, sex is not a consequence of sin but a natural act that human beings did even while in the purest paradise. Adam and Eve "had known" each other while still in a state of perfection, and sex was part of that perfection. Their sin was in disobeying God, not in having sex.

⭐ Why do you think Rashi made his comment about where Cain was conceived? How else might the story be understood?

⭐ Does Rashi's comment change what you originally thought about the story? If it does, how so?

⭐ Why do you think sex is often linked with the ideas of sin, guilt, or embarrassment?

Rape and Seeing Women as More Than Body Parts

The Bible is full of tragic stories, stories of lust, murder, and deception. One of the stories that casts a terrible light on our ancestors is the story of Dinah, the sister of all of Jacob's sons. In this case, sex leads to disastrous consequences. Sex is connected with rape, with Dinah's desire to explore the world outside her tent, to spend time with her friends. And sex is also connected to the honor of the community, which leads to deadly violence. These intense feelings about rape, about women's autonomy, and about intercommunal sex are alive in many parts of the world, leading to "honor killings." Jewish groups today do not practice honor killings, but in many Orthodox communities, if a woman is disgraced by her sexual behavior, all her brothers and sisters will suffer in being unable to find marital partners. Here is Dinah's story from the Bible:

Now Dinah, the daughter whom Leah had borne to Jacob, went out to visit the daughters of the land. Schechem the son of Hamor the Hivite, the chief of the country, saw her, and took her and lay with her by force.... Schechem said to his father Hamor, "Get me this girl as a wife".... Jacob's sons answered Schechem and his father Hamor—speaking to them with deceit because he had

defiled their sister Dinah…. "Only on this condition will
we agree with you, that you will become like us in that
every male among you is circumcised."… All the males of
the town were circumcised. On the third day, when they
were in the most pain, Simon and Levi, two of Jacob's
sons, brothers of Dinah, took each his sword, came upon
the city uncontested, and slew all the males…. They said,
"Should our sister be treated like a whore?"

(Genesis 34:1–31)

You probably did not learn about the rape of Dinah in Hebrew
school. Nor were you asked to consider the shameful behavior
of her brothers. This story is tragic on yet another level—we
never get to hear a word from Dinah. A modern reader would
accuse the sons of Jacob, Rachel, and Leah of using excessive
force in their act of revenge. And you'd probably not find anyone who would condone the use of a sacred Jewish ritual—circumcision—as a tool to weaken the enemy.[7]

- What do you think of the revenge that Simon and Levi
  undertook against the people of Shechem? Should they
  have killed the rapist? Should they have killed all the
  townsmen? Why do you think they did so? Should a
  lot of people be punished for one person's misdeeds?
- How do you think Dinah was feeling and thinking?
  What would you have wanted to happen if you
  were she? A marvelous contemporary author, Anita
  Diamant, has written the best-selling novel *The Red
  Tent* from the point of view of Dinah.
- What would you say to someone who claimed that
  Dinah brought the rape upon herself (as rape victims

are so often accused of doing)? Does any woman or girl cause her own rape?

✦ What do you think is the appropriate punishment for rape?

✦ Have you learned about "date rape," sometimes called "acquaintance rape" or "drug-facilitated sexual assault"? Being drunk or high is not an excuse to touch another person sexually, and even if a young woman is acting in a provocative way, sexual activity must always be consensual. Sexual assault and rape are terrible crimes with long-lasting effects. Always be sober and aware, be clear in your relationships, and stay with groups of people you know and trust!

What Do I Think?

How often do you think teenage guys think about sex?

_____

_____

_____

_____

_____

_____

_____

What are some of the things that scare you
about sex?

_____

_____

_____

_____

_____

_____

_____

_____

_____

_____

Have you ever watched pornography? How did you
feel about it?

_____

_____

_____

_____

Have you ever seen a young woman taken advantage of? When? How did you feel about it?

Have you had experience with a case of acquaintance rape or sexual assault? If so, what happened?

_____

_____

_____

_____

_____

_____

_____

_____

_____

_____

Do you think life is harder being gay? Why or why not?

_____

_____

_____

_____

Why do you think kids call each other "fag" or say, "That is so gay"? What can you do to make that unacceptable?

Capture any of your additional thoughts or questions here.

_____

_____

_____

_____

_____

_____

_____

_____

_____

_____

Text Connection

קְדֹשִׁים תִּהְיוּ

K'doshim tih'yu

You shall be holy.

—Leviticus 19:2

"A great idea that can inspire people can really make a difference."

"If one person can change the world, we all can."

Not on my watch

Does what I do actually matter?

לֹא תַעֲמֹד עַל־דַּם רֵעֶךָ

Lo ta'amod al dam rei'echa.

You may not stand by while
your neighbor bleeds.
—Leviticus 19:16

"One kid can make a difference by standing up, speaking out, and doing something."

"I get overwhelmed when I think about all the problems in the world."

Not on My Watch

Does what I do actually matter?

One weekend when I was a teen, I went to a friend's house, figuring that we would hang out, play video games, or play some sports in his backyard. Much to my dismay, after I got dropped off at his house, his mother said, "Keep your jacket on. We are going to serve food at a shelter!"

What? I thought. A shelter? Like, for dirty, strange people? The bums we see on the street? Aren't they hobos or something? Aren't they dangerous? How come no one told me about this before I came over? This did not feel like fun at all. I was more than a little nervous.

We parked in a lot in downtown Baltimore and entered a run-down building. There was a big room with lots of tables, the kind they had at my school cafeteria with the benches built in alongside. There was a long kitchen with a space to pass food through a divider. Inside the kitchen were a bunch of very friendly people, looking way too cheerful, considering what I thought we were doing.

My job was to bring plates of food to people. I was not prepared for what came next.

The men and women who came in were definitely unkempt but also exceedingly polite. Quietly they entered the room, took a seat, and waited. As I carried plates of spaghetti and meatballs with a side of garlic bread to their tables, almost all of them said, "Thank you" or even "God bless you." Some of the men looked quite normal, wearing clothes I could see anywhere. One man was even wearing a jacket and tie.

But what really got me was the low children's table with Sesame Street place mats on it. Mothers came in and sat near their kids as they were served. I can still picture those place mats.

When I had thought of homeless or poor people, I hadn't thought of children. I hadn't thought of mothers trying to get their children to open their mouths so they could get a spoon in. And I hadn't thought of a man wearing a jacket and tie.

I have learned a great deal since then. For example, a large number of poor people actually work but don't earn enough to make ends meet. Poor people usually are not violent; in fact, they are more often the victims of violence. In addition to direct assistance, such as food, clothing, and shelter for those in need, vulnerable people need advocates to speak out about the causes of poverty. The primary cause of homelessness is the lack of affordable housing. If we could stop thinking about accumulating wealth, we could begin to tackle the roots of this problem.

Judaism is not just about eating latkes or gefilte fish, although these are very important in creating delicious memories. It is about service for others and remembering our priorities. Most of the Jewish holidays remind us to make the world more equitable. Passover is filled with symbols to remember the enslaved, hungry Jews of Egypt. If we meet hungry people, we are instructed to empathize with them because we were once slaves in Egypt. Hanukkah is about bringing light and warmth to others during the darkest and coldest time of the year. The sukkah during the holiday of Sukkot can remind us of those who live in cardboard boxes on the streets of our cities or in tents after earthquakes or other natural disasters. Even fasting on Yom Kippur can remind us that some are hungry because they have no choice, and we can give what we would have eaten that day to a food pantry or shelter. And every time we say the *Sh'ma*—"Listen, member of the people Israel: the Eternal is our God, the Eternal is One" (Deuteronomy 6:4)—we remember that we are all interconnected, responsible for each other as part of a oneness bigger than ourselves.

Thousands of years ago people spoke out to rulers in power and demanded that the poor should not be forgotten. This act of loving-kindness would result in the world's becoming more just and compassionate. Those people were known as prophets. Prophets were outraged at the unfairness in the world and demanded that we do something about it. *Tzedakah*, or righteous giving, became a central pillar of being Jewish, as did speaking out in the name of the vulnerable.

Judaism created one of the first social justice agendas. The Torah commands us to provide food for poor and weak people (Leviticus 19:9–10). We are supposed to speak out when we see something is wrong, to "rebuke our neighbor" (Leviticus 19:17). Most important, we are supposed to greet the world with compassion and judge others favorably (*Pirkei Avot* 1:6).

But can you yourself make a difference? Even if you were to volunteer for a charity every day, would that solve the world's problems?

While you cannot single-handedly end world hunger or some other problem, the Jewish answer is yes, you can make a difference. The world has overwhelming problems: war, poverty, the environment, you name it. Choose something that matters to you, and make doing something about it a regular part of your life. The Rabbis taught, "You may not be able to complete the task, but neither are you free to desist from it" (*Pirkei Avot* 2:16).

But isn't social justice a human thing, rather than a Jewish thing? You may wonder: Should I care about whether I give to a Jewish charity as opposed to something else?

Many causes transcend our Jewish identity. You don't have to be Jewish to fight or suffer from hunger, disease, or violence. Doing good connects us all. But there are also causes that are specifically Jewish, especially those having to do with the State of Israel and helping fellow Jews.

Many Jewish families live very comfortable lives. But there are Jews all over the world who depend on Jewish charities to sustain them. Antisemitism challenges the lives of many Jews. Many people in the world, especially in the Middle East, hate Jews and the Jewish state. And despite the success of the State of Israel in tackling its own problems, challenges remain. Standing up for the worldwide Jewish community and for the State of Israel is an important form of advocacy. A very difficult fact of life is that if Jews do not give to other Jews, we cannot expect others to do so. We need to stand up for each other. *Tzedakah* must mean we care about all human beings, but we also make sure we save a special place in our efforts for the Jewish community. Rabbi Hillel taught, "If I am not for myself, who will be for me? If I am only for myself, what am I? And if not now, when?" (*Pirkei Avot* 1:14).

So the question is this: What can you do now? Whether you like it or not, your actions have effects on others, and you are responsible. Inaction is also a kind of response. What are you going to let happen on "your watch"? What single thing would you like to do improve someone else's life? Choose something and make it happen.

—RABBI JOSEPH

Find Yourself a Friend: Teen Voices

"One kid can make a difference by standing up, speaking out, and doing something."

"One person can have a huge influence. Like Martin Luther King—you can inspire people, have followers, and start change."

"If one person can change the world, we all can."

"A great idea that can inspire people can really make a difference."

"I think a person can make a difference in a lot of different ways. One could make a huge difference by starting a charity that would go on to raise millions of dollars. Or someone could make a small difference by volunteering at a food pantry. Both matter and help people. Maybe someone else would be inspired by these good deeds."

"It doesn't take much to brighten someone's day by doing something really nice for them. No matter what, you can always make a difference wherever you are and whoever you're with. Making a difference is really easy, and you can always find someone to help."

"The main things I would like to change about the world are acceptance and unity. I feel like many of the world's biggest issues are caused by racism and general hatred for each other. If the human race could work as one team to help make the best possible world to live in, most problems could be solved a lot more easily."

"I get overwhelmed when I think about all the problems in the world."

Did You Know?

- MAZON means "food" or "sustenance" in Hebrew. MAZON also refers to a nonprofit organization that works to end hunger among people of all faiths and backgrounds in the United States. As MAZON explains its mission, "Jews share a sacred duty to accept responsibility for vulnerable people in our midst." Many Jews who fast on Yom Kippur donate what they would have spent on food to organizations such as MAZON that help people who do not have enough to eat.

- While Israel is geographically far from North America, there are many ways to connect to our Jewish homeland. American Friends of Magen David Adom (MDA), for example, supports lifesaving efforts of the MDA (analogous to the Red Cross) in Israel. In fact, AFMDA provides 100 percent of the blood transfusion needs of the Israel Defense Forces and most of the ambulances and mobile intensive care units the MDA uses.

✡ Some Jewish people believe the way to make a difference is to move to Israel, join the army there, and raise a family, because the common activities of everyday life in and of themselves are building the Jewish society. The act of moving to Israel is called *aliyah*. Can you think of a connection between having an *aliyah* in synagogue and making *aliyah* to Israel? It's the same word.

✡ Animal rights is part of Jewish tradition and can be found throughout the Torah. In the Torah, often people who care for animals are heroes: King David, Moses and Jacob were all shepherds. Kosher slaughter of animals aims at minimal suffering for the livestock. And under Jewish law, animals rest on Shabbat as well.

Get Yourself a Teacher

Senator Joseph Lieberman

Making a Difference with Advocacy

Joseph Lieberman dedicated his life to public service. For over twenty-four years, Lieberman served as a U.S. senator from the state of Connecticut. In the Senate, he focused on foreign policy. Among other accomplishments from his tenure, after the 9/11 terrorist attacks he led the charge for the creation of the Department of Homeland Security. In his farewell speech to the Senate before retiring in 2013, he advised his colleagues:

Do not underestimate the impact you could have by getting involved in matters of foreign policy and national security—whether by using your voice to stand in solidarity with those who are struggling for the American ideal of freedom in their own countries across the globe, or working to strengthen the foreign policy and national security institutions of our own country, or by rallying our citizens to embrace the role that we as a country must play on the world stage, as both our interests and values demand. None of the challenges we face today, in a still dangerous world, is beyond our ability to meet.[1]

Lieberman also was the first Jew to be on an American national presidential election ticket, as the vice-presidential running mate for Al Gore. Today, even in retirement, Senator Lieberman continues to follow his own advice, advocating for timely issues, including gun control.

Sergey Brin

Making a Difference with Financial Support

How many times have you searched on Google this month, this week, or even today? Well, you can thank Sergey Brin, the Jewish immigrant from Russia who cofounded Google. The Hebrew Immigrant Aid Society (HIAS), which helps refugees of all ethnicities and religions begin new lives in the United States, brought Brin and his family to Maryland when Brin was six years old. In Russia, Brin's family suffered from antisemitism. For example, Brin's father was not able to pursue his graduate education in physics, even though he was a standout physics student. Thanks to the life-changing support from HIAS, the younger Brin was able to pursue his education in computer science and go on to change the world through his Internet innovations.

Brin gives back. He donated $1 million to HIAS, and among other causes, he is an ardent environmentalist, supporting alternative energy sources, including wind power.

Rabbi Abraham Joshua Heschel

Making a Difference through a Commitment to Equality

Polish-born American rabbi Abraham Joshua Heschel understood firsthand the painful plight of those who suffer prejudice. Many of his immediate family members were killed by Nazi persecution during the Holocaust. Committed to the value of freedom for all, including Jews, Rabbi Heschel was an activist during the civil rights movement. He marched with Rev. Dr. Martin Luther King Jr. and was outspoken about inequality, the right to vote, and poverty. Heschel found racism especially offensive, thinking it violated central lessons of protecting the weak and not being prejudiced, which are at the heart of the story of the Exodus from Egypt. He explained:

> At the first conference on religion and race, the main participants were Pharaoh and Moses.... The outcome of that summit meeting has not come to an end. Pharaoh is not ready to capitulate. The exodus began, but is far from having been completed.... To think of [humanity] in terms of white, black, or yellow is more than an error. *It is an eye disease, a cancer of the soul....* How many disasters do we have to go through in order to realize

that all of humanity has a stake in the liberty of one person; whenever one person is offended, we are all hurt. What begins as inequality of some inevitably ends as inequality of all.[2]

Learn

The Prophets

The First Social Justice Activists

The prophets felt God was angry when people would come to worship at the Temple in Jerusalem with sacrifices but then went home and did unjust things. In other words, if you go to synagogue to pray and say an unkind word to a homeless person on your way there, you have missed the point of synagogue. Here are some of the prophets' words:

Wash yourselves; cleanse yourselves, put your evil doings away from My sight. Cease to do evil, learn to do good, seek justice; relieve the oppressed. Uphold the orphan's rights; take up the widow's cause.

(Isaiah 1:16–17)

For learning shall come forth from Zion, the word of the Eternal from Jerusalem. Thus God will judge among the nations and arbitrate for the many peoples, and they shall beat their swords into plowshares and their spears into pruning hooks: nation shall not take up sword against nation; they shall never again know war.

(Isaiah 2:3–4)

Is this such a fast I desire, a day for people to starve their bodies? Is it bowing the head like a reed and lying in sackcloth and ashes? Do you call that a fast, a day when the Eternal is happy? No, this is the fast I desire: To unlock fetters of wickedness, and untie the cords of the load, to let the oppressed go free, to break off every burden. It is to share your bread with the hungry, and to take the wretched poor into your home; when you see the naked, to clothe him, and not to ignore your own kin.

(Isaiah 58:5–7)

Seek what is good and not what is evil so that you may live.... See that justice is done in the courts.... Let justice roll down like waters, righteousness as a mighty stream.

(Amos 5:14, 5:15, 5:24)

I desire loving-kindness and not sacrifice, attachment to God rather than burnt offerings.

(Hosea 6:6)

With what shall I come before the Eternal, and bow myself before God on high? Shall I come before God with burnt offerings, with calves a year old? Will the Eternal be pleased with thousands of rams, with ten thousand rivers of oil?... God has shown you, O mortal, what is good, and what the Eternal requires of you: Only to do justice, to love kindness, and to walk humbly with your God.

(Micah 6:6–8)

⭐ Identify some of the problems the prophets were criticizing in society. What did they say was offensive to God?

⭐ Which of these quotations speaks to you the most?
Why?

⭐ If you were to identify a modern-day prophet, who
would it be? Why? Is there anyone living today who
you think qualifies?

Moses Maimonides's Rules on How to Give to a Poor Person

Never has anyone become poor by giving *tzedakah*,
nor has anything bad ever come of it.... Those who
avert their eyes from [the need of] *tzedakah* are called
"cruel." ... Those who give *tzedakah* to the poor with a
scowl and cause them to be embarrassed, even if they
gave them a thousand coins, have destroyed and lost any
merit thereby. Rather, one should give cheerfully, with
happiness [to do so] and empathy for their plight....
And one should speak to them words of comfort and
consolation.... If a poor person asks you [to give him or
her something], and you do not have anything in your
possession to give to him or her, comfort the person with
words. It is forbidden to speak harshly to the poor or to
raise your voice in a shout, for their hearts are broken
and crushed.

(Maimonides, *Mishneh Torah*, **Laws of Gifts to the Poor 10**)

 Moses Maimonides wanted people to act a certain way
if they saw a beggar on the street. What are his main
rules for conduct?

⭐ Why do you think he wrote that if you give something
with "a scowl," you have lost any merit in giving?

⭐ Why do you think Maimonides says that if you don't have anything to give, you should still say something comforting? Do you think you would be comfortable doing so?

⭐ If you see a beggar on the street, would you give him or her a dollar? Why or why not? What are some alternatives to giving on the street?

A Prayer by Rabbi Jack Riemer

We cannot merely pray to You, O God, to end war;
for we know that You have made the world in a way
that we must find our own paths to peace
within ourselves and with our neighbors.

We cannot merely pray to You, O God,
to end starvation;
for You have already given us the resources
with which to feed the entire world,
if we would only use them wisely.

We cannot merely pray to You, O God,
to root out prejudice;
for You have already given us eyes
with which to see the good in others,
if we would only use them rightly.

We cannot merely pray to You, O God, to end despair;
for You have already given us the power
to clear away slums and to give hope,
if we would only use our power justly.

We cannot merely pray to You, O God, to end disease;
for You have already given us great minds

with which to search out cures and healings,
if we would only use them constructively.

Therefore, we pray to You instead, O God,
for strength, determination, and will power,
to *do* instead of just to pray,
to *become* instead of merely to wish,

for Your sake and for ours, speedily and soon,
that our land and our world may be safe,
and that our lives may be blessed.[3]

✡ Where is God when so many people are messing up the world? This prayer tries to answer that question. What is this prayer's answer?

✡ This prayer imagines a partnership between people and God. What is God's part in making the world? What is our part?

✡ Have you ever thought of the connection between praying and doing? Is it enough just to pray?

What Do I Think?

How do you think one person can make a difference?

_____

_____

_____

_____

_____

_____

_____

_____

What has someone done for you or to you that you
really appreciated? Did it cost them anything—
time, money, or risk—to help you?

_____

_____

_____

_____

_____

_____

_____

_____

_____

_____

If you had a magic wand, what would be the first
thing you would change in the world?

_____

_____

_____

_____

_____

_____

_____

_____

Capture any of your additional thoughts or questions
here.

_____

_____

_____

_____

_____

_____

_____

_____

_____

_____

_____

Text Connection

לֹא תַעֲמֹד עַל־דַּם רֵעֶךָ

Lo ta'amod al dam rei'echa.

You may not stand by while your neighbor bleeds.

—Leviticus 19:16

"My dad is always selfless, doing things for the rest of his family before himself."

"I would like to improve my humility. I'm not very humble, but I've been working on it, and I think I see an improvement."

Looking inside at the man I want to be

Beginning with myself.

מִצְוָה גוֹרֶרֶת מִצְוָה, וַעֲבֵרָה גוֹרֶרֶת עֲבֵרָה

Mitzvah goreret mitzvah, va'aveirah goreret aveirah.

One *mitzvah* will bring another *mitzvah*, one sin will bring another sin.

—*Pirkei Avot* 4:2

"I think I try to be funny too much. And I need to always remember to judge people by what's on the inside."

"I can give more kindness to the people in my life."

Looking Inside at the Man I Want to Be

Beginning with myself.

Many people receive a *tallit*, or prayer shawl, as a present when they become a bar mitzvah. Mine is a "Joseph's coat" *tallit*. It has many colors going down the sides. My mother picked out this *tallit* from all the rest because my name is Joseph. I enjoy wearing my *tallit* not only because it is colorful and meaningful, but also because it gives me something to fiddle with during services—the *tzitzit*, the fringes hanging from the corners, the most important part of the *tallit*.

The *tzitzit* are tied in a specific way. On each fringe are five knots, recalling the Torah, the Five Books of Moses. Look closely, and you will see the five knots are actually double knots, which symbolize the Ten Commandments. From the knots dangle eight threads, symbolizing the eighth day of the covenant of circumcision for a baby boy. When we see these knots and threads, we are supposed to remember God and the *mitzvot* (commandments).

Some define *mitzvah* as a "good deed," or as something nice that you do—if you have the time. *Mitzvah*, however, literally means "divine commandment." It is something God *wants* you to do.

The Rabbis teach that "one *mitzvah* will bring another *mitzvah*, one sin will bring another sin" (*Pirkei Avot* 4:2). The choices we make affect our future choices and influence other people to do the same. We develop habits. If we carry out *mitzvot* regularly, we develop positive habits that make us into what in Yiddish is called a *mensch*, a decent human being. Everyone should want to be a *mensch* and surround themselves with other good people.

Sometimes we need help to push us in the right direction. Let me tell you the day that I learned the meaning of *mitzvah*.

It happened when I was growing up in Maryland. It was a snowy day. As my mother and I were driving up to the house, we noticed our neighbor, Mr. Mercier, chopping ice off his driveway.

"Go out and help him," my mother said. I began to complain that I didn't feel like it.

Oops.

About half a second later, my mother stopped the car, turned to face me, and kicked me out. As I was flying out the car door, she said, "Do it because it's a *mitzvah!*"

Sometimes, a *mitzvah* comes with a kick in the rear.

The *tzitzit* are supposed to be like a string tied around your finger (or a kick in the rear), reminding you to do God's commandments—even if you don't feel like it. They symbolize our responsibilities to others—whether they live next door, in the next bedroom, or in the next country.

With our new, contemporary knowledge, the fringes of the *tallit* take on even deeper meaning. In the twenty-first century, scientists overwhelmingly accept the big bang theory—how the universe originated at one point in space and time. They also endorse Charles Darwin's concept of evolution, how all living things on our planet go back to one original organism with a particular DNA structure. This means we are all connected because we were all originally one, coming from the same starting point. Over millions of years we have evolved from single-cell organisms to the complicated creatures we are today.

Similarly, if we look at the *tzitzit*, we can see how they are all knotted and tied together. The strings and knots can remind us of the interconnectedness of all things, our connections with each other, and our relationships and responsibilities: the "ties that bind." Each of us is the end of a dangling thread going back to the same Source.

You are connected to people and nature. The people who grow your food, who deliver and package it, and who put it on your table; the electricity that comes to your home, and the impulses that run through your nerves; the water that comes through the pipes, and the blood in your arteries; the tree breathing through its leaves, and you breathing through your lungs; the person writing you a note from the chair next to you, and the person driving away your trash; the teenager in the car and the man on the driveway—everything and everyone are interdependent. We are tied to and affect one another.

We are also tied to the people who came before us and those who will come after us. We all go back to a common ancestor (whom we can call Adam, if we want), and even before that—to a single point of extraordinary light that exploded ("Let there be light").

The *tzitzit* remind us of what we should do for each other, because we are irrevocably tied together. If we are the threads, then God is the Knot.

Your job is to be a *mensch*, a decent human being. You are supposed to remember that you are connected to and are responsible for the people and the planet. To help you, the *mitzvot* form a "*mensch* manual" for you to follow. Consider them a code for ethical Jewish behavior. And Jewish rituals, like wearing a *tallit*, serve as a reminder to bring you back to that code when you forget or get lost along the way.

Begin with yourself: If you want to improve the world, you have to make sure you are living up to your own ideals. Believe it or not, just by making a change in yourself, you can be an inspiration to others.[1]

—RABBI JOSEPH

Find Yourself a Friend: Teen Voices

"People all want to do the right thing,
but sometimes people don't think or
they can't discern right from wrong."

"I would like to improve my humility. I'm
not very humble, but I've been working on
it, and I think I see an improvement."

"My dad is my role model because he is
always there to help me, whether it is
physically or just talking on the phone."

"I think I try to be funny too much. And
I need to always remember to judge
people by what's on the inside."

"I think a small step I can take to become
more of the person I want to be is to
be polite to everyone and just smile."

"My family tries to beat kindness into my brain.
They tell personal stories, connections, and rants
about who I am and where I come from."

"One good thing about me is my
determination to accomplish a task."

"I can give more kindness to
the people in my life."

" *I would like to learn to be
nicer and more welcoming.*"

"My dad is always selfless, doing things for
the rest of his family before himself."

" *I would like to improve the way I treat
my younger brother. Even though he is so
annoying, I still shouldn't be as mean.*"

"Something I would like to improve about
myself is that I am generally lazy. I
procrastinate with work, and I try to scrape
by in school, getting along with good grades
but minimal effort. I think if I put a little
more effort into things, I will be more willing
to help people and be a little less lazy."

Did You Know?

⭐ The Yiddish word for a decent human being is
mensch. Menschlichkeit means the characteristics that
make someone a *mensch* or things that bring more
kindness into the world. Despite the first three letters,
mensch refers to both men and women of high moral
character. Surrounding yourself with good people
helps you have a good life.

⭐ Another important Jewish concept is *derech eretz,*
meaning "being civil." Literally *derech eretz* means
the way (*derech*) of the land (or community) (*eretz*).

This concept is so important that entire books have been written about it. *Derech eretz* refers to the millions of small acts that reflect your character, such as stopping to help someone who has dropped something, not making a lot of noise that would disturb others, not cutting in line, not accepting the wrong change after a purchase, and so on. British rabbi Julian Sinclair wrote an article about what *derech eretz* means.[2] According to Rabbi Sinclair, it's something like good manners. For example, if there's no other firm reason for disapproving of something, you might say, "It's just not *derech eretz*." *Derech eretz* covers the basic norms of decent human behavior that the Torah teaches. Living according to *derech eretz* is so important that there is a saying, "*Derech eretz* comes before Torah." Examples Rabbi Sinclair gives are speaking calmly and gently to people; eating sitting down like a human being, rather than while walking in the street, like an animal; dressing in clothes that are clean and presentable, but not gaudy or extravagant; walking naturally rather than pretentiously or affectedly; and generally behaving like a respectful and sensitive person.

Athletes competing in the Maccabee Games, the international Jewish Community Center–sponsored youth Olympics, take time out to perform community service projects. Recent projects have included beautifying neighborhood facilities, spending time with elders in nursing homes, and visiting children and teens who are in local hospitals.

Get Yourself a Teacher

Ohio State University Hillel Students

The Mitzvah of Saving a Life

Part of being Jewish means doing good in the world. Ohio State University students involved in a national Jewish college organization called Hillel took this Jewish concept to heart. They partnered with the Gift of Life Bone Marrow Foundation to organize drives to register bone marrow donation volunteers. Since Jewish donors are underrepresented in the national bone marrow registry, it is more difficult to find a match for Jewish people who have leukemia and need a bone marrow transplant than it is for other ethnic and religious groups. Incredibly, one Ohio State student was found to be a match for a two-year-old Jewish girl diagnosed with leukemia. The college student donated his marrow—giving the precious gift of life, of survival. Since 2001, eighty-five Hillel organizations across different college campuses have recruited 26,541 bone marrow donors, yielding 937 matches. The Talmud says that saving a single life is like saving the world.

Danny Siegel

Helping Mitzvah Heroes Make a Bigger Impact

Danny Siegel is an author, poet, and widely admired *tzedakah* leader. For more than thirty years, Siegel has raised and given away more than $13 million to people who help others. Growing up active in his Jewish community and United Synagogue

Youth, Siegel saw firsthand the many acts of kindness performed by his congregation and by his dad, a country doctor who made house calls. Inspired to help others, Siegel at first asked friends and family to donate money for Siegel to give to people making a difference in Israel. He became so respected for his ability to identify worthy organizations that in 1981 he launched a charity called the Ziv Tzedakah Fund. The fund gave money to "*mitzvah* heroes," people and groups already doing good deeds, but who could do even more good if they had more money. Danny Siegel believes *mitzvah* heroes are role models we should help: "*Mitzvah* heroes are everywhere—both sexes, every age (the ones I have met are from ages seven to ninety-eight), every body shape ... gorgeous or plain as can be." One of his favorite quotes is from Abraham Joshua Heschel: "When I was young, I admired clever people. As I grew old, I came to admire kind people." Siegel is a great example of a *mitzvah* hero himself.

Frank Nikbakht

Helping Give a Voice to Those Unable to Speak Up

For nearly twenty years, Frank Nikbakht has worked to expose Iranian human rights violations against Jews, Christians, Zoroastrians, other non-Muslims, and women. Born in Tehran, he escaped from Iran in 1982 when he was twenty-nine. Nikbakht lives in southern California, where he leads a volunteer effort to increase public awareness of the persecution suffered by religious minorities and women in Iran. Under Iranian law, non-Muslims are second-class citizens with limited rights. Women also face extreme discrimination in Iran. Iranian leadership has infamously denied that the Holocaust ever occurred. Jews living in Iran today exist under a cloud of fear, not able to speak out publicly about the hardships they experience. Nikbakht has not forgotten his roots. He uses the freedom of the American press, which we often take for granted, to voice concerns of those minorities who cannot speak out for themselves in Iran.

Anonymous

Helping with an Outstretched Arm

Sometimes an act of kindness has an unexpected, even more powerful impact. On the morning of September 11, 2001, a recent college graduate, Usman Farman, born in Pakistan and a Muslim, was commuting by train to his job in New York City. His train entered the World Trade Center stop shortly before nine o'clock, when suddenly there was a groundshaking explosion. The South Tower of the World Trade Center was collapsing just blocks away as a result of Islamist terrorists flying a plane into the building. The explosion knocked Farman down, and he landed flat on his back. Caught in the chaotic stampede to escape, his life might have ended right there on the ground. But a Hasidic man fleeing the turmoil saw Farman, leaned down, saw the Muslim prayer on the pendant Farman wore around his neck, and then held out his hand, saying in a strong New York accent, "Brother, if you don't mind, there's a cloud of glass coming at us. Grab my hand, let's get the hell out of here." Although Farman was never able to identify his rescuer, ever grateful, he shared his story with the president of his alma mater, all his friends, and fortunately with CNN, so he could let people know about the anonymous Jew who saved his life.

Learn

Here is a list of *mitzvot* and customs from the Torah and Jewish tradition.

Put a ✔ next to a commandment you currently do or try to do.

Put an ✘ next to a commandment you have no interest in.

Put a ❓ next to a commandment you do not understand or you are not sure applies to you in your life at this time.

You may be surprised to learn that your life is already filled with *mitzvot*.

Beliefs

Sh'ma: believing God is one, the unity of all (Exodus 20:2; Deuteronomy 6:4)

B'tzelem Elohim: acknowledging that all people are made in God's image and are uniquely special (Genesis 1:27)

Lo yih'yeh elohim acherim: not to put faith in other gods, idols, or things (Exodus 20:3)

Ethics and *Tikkun Olam* (Repairing the World)

V'ahavta l'rei'acha kamocha: loving your neighbor as yourself; "What is hateful to you, do not do to your neighbor" (Leviticus 19:18; Talmud, *Shabbat* 31a)

Lo tirtzach; lo ta'amod al dam rei'echa; pikuach nefesh: not to murder; not stand by while your neighbor bleeds; saving life (Exodus 20:13; Leviticus 18:5, 19:16)

Lo tisa et shem Adonai Elohecha lashav: not to swear an oath falsely in God's name (Exodus 20:7)

Lo tinaf: not to commit adultery (Exodus 20:13)

Lo tignov: not to steal (Exodus 20:13)

Lo ta'aneh v'rei'acha eid shaker: not to lie or bear false witness (Exodus 20:13)

Lo tachmod: not to covet (Exodus 20:14)

Tzedakah: acts of philanthropy (Exodus 22:24; Leviticus 19:10, 23:22; Deuteronomy 24:19)

Hochei'ach tochiach: acts of protest and rebuke (Leviticus 19:17)

Bal tashchit: not to destroy unnecessarily (Deuteronomy 20:19)

Rodef shalom: pursuing peace in the world (Leviticus 19:18; Deuteronomy 16:20, 20:10)

Shalom bayit: seeking peace in the home and family (Exodus 20:12; Leviticus 19:3; Deuteronomy 6:7)

Kavod: showing respect, but especially to honor one's parent(s), the elderly, teachers, and the dead (Genesis

1:27, 5:1–2; Exodus 20:12; Leviticus 19:32; Numbers 27:20; Deuteronomy 34:6)

Hachnasat orchim: welcoming the stranger; including others (Genesis 18:2)

Sh'mirat halashon: avoiding hurtful speech (Leviticus 19:16)

Tzar baalei chayim: not causing needless pain to any creature (Deuteronomy 22:6–7, 25:4)

Bikur cholim: visiting the sick (Genesis 18:1; Numbers 12:13)

Holiday Traditions

Shabbat: observing a day of peace each week among family and community and refraining from labor (Exodus 20:8–10; Leviticus 23:3)

Rosh Hashanah: hearing the shofar proclaim the New Year (Leviticus 23:24)

Yom Kippur: fasting, repentance, self-reflection (Leviticus 23:27–32)

Sukkot and *Shemini Atzeret:* dwelling in a sukkah, waving the *lulav* and *etrog* (Leviticus 23:34–36)

Simchat Torah: hearing the ending and beginning of the Torah and carrying the Torah scroll (Leviticus 23:36; *Tur* and *Shulchan Aruch, Orach Chayim* 669)

Chanukkah: displaying the light of the menorah and celebrating religious freedom (Talmud, *Shabbat* 21b)

Tu Bish'vat: planting trees in Israel and respecting the environment (Talmud, *Rosh Hashanah* 14b–15b)

Purim: hearing the *megillah* of Esther, rejoicing, and sending food to friends and the poor (Esther 9:20–22)

Pesach: getting rid of leaven, participating in a seder, eating matzah and *maror*, and not eating *chametz* for a week (Leviticus 23:5–8)

Shavuot: witnessing the recital of the Ten Commandments (Leviticus 23:15–21)

Tisha B'Av: fasting in commemoration of the destruction of the Temple and other disasters of Jewish history (Talmud, *Ta'anit* 11b–13a)

Life-Cycle Traditions

B'rit milah / simchat bat: covenant of circumcision for boys and naming for girls (Genesis 17:11–13)

Bar/bat mitzvah: coming of age (*Pirkei Avot* 5:21)

Chuppah: marriage (Exodus 21:10; Deuteronomy 24:1)

Aveilut: mourning through *shiva*, *sh'loshim*, and *yahrzeit* (Genesis 23:1–4, 50:10; Numbers 20:29)

Everyday Holiness

Talmud Torah: studying Torah (Deuteronomy 4:9, 6:6–7)

T'filah: prayer and meditation (Genesis 8:20, 12:7–8; Deuteronomy 8:10, etc.)

Kashrut: ritual consumption, mindful eating (Leviticus 11; Deuteronomy 14:3–21)

T'shuvah: apologizing and forgiving, returning to and reconnecting with God and each other, repentance and changing your behavior (Leviticus 23:28; Numbers 5:6–7)

G'milut chasadim: acts of loving-kindness (Exodus 34:6–7)

- ✡ What on the list is most important to you? Least important? Why?
- ✡ What commandments and customs do you think are the minimum for you to feel that you have a Jewish identity?
- ✡ What commandments and customs do you think are the minimum to ensure a Jewish future?

Moses Maimonides: The Middle Path

Good acts are those midway between two extremes that are bad, namely, too much and too little....

Generosity is midway between being cheap and overindulgence.

Courage is midway between recklessness and cowardice.

Self-confidence is midway between arrogance and embarrassment.

Dignity is midway between being bossy and being submissive....

Humility is midway between pride and shame....

In truth, it is the middle way that is best.[3]

> ✡ What is Maimonides trying to teach about a life of healthy emotional balance? How does this effect your efforts to be the kind of person you want to be?
>
> ✡ What are some ways you think you go to extremes? What is the result?
>
> ✡ Are there times when being extreme for something is a good thing? How or when?

Who Is an Ideal Man?

Ben Zoma taught:
Who is wise? The person who learns from everyone.
Who is strong? The man who controls his urges.
Who is wealthy? The one who is happy with what he has.
Who is honored? He who honors others.

(Pirkei Avot 4:1)

We might be tempted to measure wisdom by what grades we get or titles we earn. We think of strength in terms of muscles or power. We think of wealth in terms of money, and honor in terms of fame. The sage Ben Zoma is teaching something else.

- Who in your life represents wisdom?
- Strength?
- Wealth?
- Social respect?
- How would you define "success"?

What Do I Think?

Who is a role model of a kind, decent man in your life? Why do you think so?

_____

_____

_____

_____

_____

_____

_____

_____

_____

_____

_____

What are some qualities you are most proud of in your character?

_____

_____

_____

_____

_____

_____

_____

_____

_____

_____

What are some qualities you would like to improve?

_____

_____

_____

_____

_____

What is one small step you can take to become more of the person you want to be?

Capture any of your additional thoughts or questions here.

_____

_____

_____

_____

_____

_____

_____

_____

_____

Text Connection

מִצְוָה גוֹרֶרֶת מִצְוָה, וַעֲבֵרָה גוֹרֶרֶת עֲבֵרָה

Mitzvah goreret mitzvah, va'aveirah goreret aveirah.

One *mitzvah* will bring another *mitzvah*,
one sin will bring another sin.

—*Pirkei Avot* 4:2

Notes

Courage

1. *Merriam-Webster*, www.merriam-webster.com/dictionary/courage.
2. Empowering Jews with Disabilities, http://empoweringjews-withdisabilities.blogspot.com/2012_03_01_archive.html.
3. Ibid.

Frenemies

1. Dan Kindlon and Michael Thompson, *Raising Cain* (New York: Random House, 1999), 72–75
2. Simcha Raz, *The Sayings of Menahem Mendel of Kotzk*, trans. Edward Levin (Northvale, NJ: Jason Aronson, 1995), 70.
3. Gal Beckerman, *When They Come for Us We'll Be Gone: The Epic Struggle to Save Soviet Jewry* (New York: Houghton Mifflin Harcourt, 2010).
4. Dotson Rader, "Daniel Radcliffe's Life after Harry," *Parade*, January 7, 2012, www.parade.com/celebrity/celebrity-parade/2012/01/life-after-harry.html; Craig McLean, "Dan the Man," *Guardian*, July 3, 2009, www.guardian.co.uk/film/2009/jul/04/daniel-radcliffe-harry-potter-jk-rowling.
5. "Daniel Radcliffe Offers Support to US Charity Helping Suicidal Gays," *Telegraph*, August 12, 2009, www.telegraph.co.uk/news/celebritynews/6012328/Daniel-Radcliffe-offers-support-to-US-charity-helping-suicidal-gays.html.
6. Hilary Leila Krieger, "Strategic Ties Vital to US and Israel," *Jerusalem Post*, April 16, 2010, http://www.jpost.com/International/Strategic-ties-vital-to-US-and-Israel.
7. Micah Hendler, LinkedIn profile, www.linkedin.com/profile/view?id=137337759&authType=NAME_SEARCH&authToken=1Vla&locale=en_US&srchid=25234313695

17132764&srchindex=1&srchtotal=1&trk=vsrp_people_res_name
&trkInfo=VSRPsearchId%3A2523431369517132764%2CVSRPtarg
etId%3A137337759%2CVSRPcmpt%3Aprimary.

8. Chaim Potok, *The Chosen* (New York: Simon and Schuster, 1967), 71.

True to Myself

1. Jewish Virtual Library, www.jewishvirtuallibrary.org/jsource/ biography/sharansky.html.
2. Chet Cooper, "Howie Mandel: Can't Touch This!," *Ability Magazine*, June/July 2011, http://abilitymagazine.com/Howie-Mandel. html.
3. Daniel Smith, *Monkey Mind: A Memoir of Anxiety* (New York: Simon & Schuster, 2012) 143–144.
4. Ibid., 144.
5. Adapted from Arthur Green, *Ehyeh: A Kabbalah for Tomorrow* (Woodstock, VT: Jewish Lights Publishing, 2003), 127–130

One Day, Son, This Will All Be Yours

1. "Stay-at-Home Dad," *Wikipedia*, http://en.wikipedia.org/wiki/ stay-at-home_dad.
2. www.andamsandler.com (accessed July 12, 2012).
3. Jessica E. Vascellaro, "Using YouTube for Posterity," *Wall Street Journal*, May 10, 2007, excerpted in www.press.feedmebubbe.com/ press/?tag=wall-street-journal.
4. W. Gunther Plant, ed., *The Torah: A Modern Commentary*, rev. ed. (New York: URJ Press, 2005), 142.

God ... Really?

1. "In 1983, the Reform movement made a patrilineal descent ruling. The Reform movement decided to accept the children of Jewish fathers as Jews even without a conversion ceremony. In addition, the movement decided to accept people who were raised as Jews, such as adopted children, even if it was not certain that either of their parents were Jewish" (http://judaism.about.com/od/ whoisajew/a/whoisjewdescent.htm).

2. *New York Times*, April 19, 1955, www.nytimes.com/learning/ general/onthisday/bday/0314.html.

The Torah of Everything

1. Abraham Joshua Heschel, *God in Search of Man* (Philadelphia: Jewish Publication Society, 1959), 46.
2. Adapted from Martin Buber, *The Way of Man: According to Hasidic Teaching* (Woodstock, VT: Jewish Lights, 2012).
3. Translation adapted from Daniel Matt, *The Essential Kabbalah* (Edison, NJ: Castle Books, 1997), 24.

Enough Already

1. "APA Survey Raises Concern about Health Impact of Stress on Children and Families," November 9, 2010; www.apa.org/news/ press/releases/2010/11/stress-in-america.aspx.
2. Nishmaat Hayyim: Jewish Meditation Community, www.tbz-brookline.org/resources/meditation/nishmat-hayyim/.
3. *Baltimore Jewish Times* (December 28, 2012): 42.
4. Festival of Faith and Music, Calvin College, www.calvin.edu/ admin/sao/festival/2011/concerts/matisyahu.php.
5. Abraham Joshua Heschel, *The Sabbath* (New York: Farrar, Straus and Giroux, 1951), 13, 28.

Falling in Lust, Falling in Love

1. This list was produced by the Ad Hoc Committee on Human Sexuality of the Central Conference of American Rabbis in June 1998. While it comes from the Reform movement, these values transcend any single denomination. It can be found here: http://huc.edu/ijso/docs/1998%20Ad-Hoc%20Committee%20Report%20on%20Human%20Sexuality.pdf.
2. Barbara Greenberg, "Oral Sex Is the New Bar Mitzvah Present?," *Psychology Today*, October 15, 2011, www.psychologytoday. com/blog/the-teen-doctor/201110/oral-sex-is-the-new-bar-mitzvah-present-0.
3. Emily Shire, "Hooking Up at Summer Camp," *Forward*, August 17, 2012, Forward.com/articles/161165/hooking-up-at-summer-camp/?p=all.

4. Richard N. Ostling, "Giving the Talmud to the Jews," *Time* (January 18, 1988).

5. "Dr. Ruth Asks: What Is Sex For?," The Big Questions, Global Day of Jewish Learning, www.theglobalday.com/what-is-sex-for/.

6. Amos Oz, *A Tale of Love and Darkness* (Orlando, FL: Harcourt, 2003), 112–114.

7. This text and these questions deliberately overlap with *The JGirl's Guide: A Young Jewish Woman's Handbook for Coming of Age* (Woodstock, VT: Jewish Lights, 2005), 113–114. In a classroom setting, this might be an opportunity for a joint session.

Not on My Watch

1. Alana Goodman, "Joe Lieberman's Farewell Speech," *Commentary*, December 13, 2012, www.commentarymagazine. com/2012/12/13/joe-liebermans-farewell-speech/.

2. Abraham Joshua Heschel, *The Insecurity of Freedom* (New York: First Noonday Press, 1967; first eBook edition, 2011).

3. *Likrat Shabbat: Worship, Study and Song for Sabbath and Festival Evenings* (Bridgeport, CT: Media Judaica, 1992) 123.

Looking Inside at the Man I Want to Be

1. A version of this section was first published in Jeffrey Salkin, ed., *Text Messages: A Torah Commentary for Teens* (Woodstock, VT: Jewish Lights, 2012), 250.

2. Julian Sinclair, "Derech Eretz," *Jewish Chronicle Online*, November 5, 2008, www.thejc.com/judaism.jewish-words/derech-eretz.

3. Translation adapted from Leonard Kravitz and Kerry M. Olitzky, *Shemonah Perakim: A Treatise on the Soul* (New York: UAHC Press, 1999), 33–35, 38.

Suggestions for Further Learning

Learning to be a Jewish man never stops. This GPS guides you to only a few stops on the journey. Here are some other books you might want to check out to keep exploring further down the road.

Feinstein, Edward. *Tough Questions Jews Ask: A Young Adult's Guide to Building a Jewish Life.* 2nd ed. Woodstock, VT: Jewish Lights Publishing, 2011.

Mack, Stan. *The Story of the Jews: A 4,000 Year Adventure—A Graphic History Book.* Woodstock VT: Jewish Lights Publishing, 2001.

Oseary, Guy, Ben Stiller, and Perry Farrell. *Jews Who Rock.* New York: St. Martin's Press, 2001.

Pearl, Judea and Ruth, eds. *I Am Jewish: Personal Reflections Inspired by the Last Words of Daniel Pearl.* Woodstock VT: Jewish Lights Publishing, 2005.

Salkin, Jeffrey. *For Kids—Putting God on Your Guest List. How to Claim the Spiritual Meaning of Your Bar or Bat Mitzvah.* 2nd ed. Woodstock VT: Jewish Lights Publishing, 2007.

———, ed. *Text Messages: A Torah Commentary for Teens.* Woodstock, VT: Jewish Lights Publishing, 2012.

Sheinkin, Steve. *The Adventures of Rabbi Harvey: A Graphic Novel of Jewish Wisdom and Wit in the Wild West.* Woodstock, VT: Jewish Lights Publishing, 2006.

———. *Rabbi Harvey Rides Again: A Graphic Novel of Jewish Folktales Let Loose in the Wild West.* Woodstock, VT: Jewish Lights Publishing, 2008.

————. *Rabbi Harvey vs. the Wisdom Kid: A Graphic Novel of Dueling Jewish Folktales in the Wild West*. Woodstock, VT: Jewish Lights Publishing, 2010.

Slater, Robert. *Great Jews in Sports*. New York: Jonathan David Publishers, 2005.

Suneby, Liz, and Diane Heiman. *The Mitzvah Project Book: Making Mitzvah Part of Your Bar/Bat Mitzvah and Your Life*. Woodstock, VT: Jewish Lights Publishing, 2011.

Wolfson, Ron. *God's To-do List: 103 Ways to Be an Angel and Do God's Work on Earth*. Woodstock VT: Jewish Lights Publishing, 2006.

My Notes

My Notes

My Notes

My Notes

Bible Study / Midrash

Passing Life's Tests: Spiritual Reflections on the Trial of Abraham, the Binding of Isaac *By Rabbi Bradley Shavit Artson, DHL*
Invites us to use this powerful tale as a tool for our own soul wrestling, to confront our existential sacrifices and enable us to face—and surmount—life's tests.
6 x 9, 176 pp, Quality PB, 978-1-58023-631-7 **$18.99**

The Messiah and the Jews: Three Thousand Years of Tradition, Belief and Hope *By Rabbi Elaine Rose Glickman; Foreword by Rabbi Neil Gillman, PhD; Preface by Rabbi Judith Z. Abrams, PhD*
Explores and explains an astonishing range of primary and secondary sources, infusing them with new meaning for the modern reader.
6 x 9, 192 pp, Quality PB, 978-1-58023-690-4 **$16.99**

Speaking Torah: Spiritual Teachings from around the Maggid's Table—in Two Volumes *By Arthur Green, with Ebn Leader, Ariel Evan Mayse and Or N. Rose*
The most powerful Hasidic teachings made accessible—from some of the world's preeminent authorities on Jewish thought and spirituality.
Volume 1—6 x 9, 512 pp, Hardcover, 978-1-58023-668-3 **$34.99**
Volume 2—6 x 9, 448 pp, Hardcover, 978-1-58023-694-2 **$34.99**

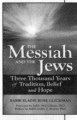

Masking and Unmasking Ourselves: Interpreting Biblical Texts on Clothing & Identity *By Dr. Norman J. Cohen*
Presents ten Bible stories that involve clothing in an essential way, as a means of learning about the text, its characters and their interactions.
6 x 9, 240 pp, HC, 978-1-58023-461-0 **$24.99**

The Genesis of Leadership: What the Bible Teaches Us about Vision, Values and Leading Change *By Rabbi Nathan Laufer; Foreword by Senator Joseph I. Lieberman*
6 x 9, 288 pp, Quality PB, 978-1-58023-352-1 **$18.99**

Hineini in Our Lives: Learning How to Respond to Others through 14 Biblical Texts and Personal Stories *By Rabbi Norman J. Cohen, PhD* 6 x 9, 240 pp, Quality PB, 978-1-58023-274-6 **$16.99**

The Modern Men's Torah Commentary: New Insights from Jewish Men on the 54 Weekly Torah Portions *Edited by Rabbi Jeffrey K. Salkin*
6 x 9, 368 pp, HC, 978-1-58023-395-8 **$24.99**

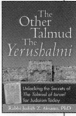

Moses and the Journey to Leadership: Timeless Lessons of Effective Management from the Bible and Today's Leaders *By Rabbi Norman J. Cohen, PhD*
6 x 9, 240 pp, Quality PB, 978-1-58023-351-4 **$18.99**; HC, 978-1-58023-227-2 **$21.99**

The Other Talmud—*The Yerushalmi:* Unlocking the Secrets of The Talmud of Israel for Judaism Today *By Rabbi Judith Z. Abrams, PhD*
6 x 9, 256 pp, HC, 978-1-58023-463-4 **$24.99**

Sage Tales: Wisdom and Wonder from the Rabbis of the Talmud
By Rabbi Burton L. Visotzky 6 x 9, 256 pp, HC, 978-1-58023-456-6 **$24.99**

The Torah Revolution: Fourteen Truths That Changed the World
By Rabbi Reuven Hammer, PhD 6 x 9, 240 pp, HC, 978-1-58023-457-3 **$24.99**

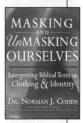

The Wisdom of Judaism: An Introduction to the Values of the Talmud
By Rabbi Dov Peretz Elkins 6 x 9, 192 pp, Quality PB, 978-1-58023-327-9 **$16.99**

Or phone, fax, mail or e-mail to: **JEWISH LIGHTS Publishing**
Sunset Farm Offices, Route 4 • P.O. Box 237 • Woodstock, Vermont 05091
Tel: (802) 457-4000 • Fax: (802) 457-4004 • www.jewishlights.com
Credit card orders: (800) 962-4544 (8:30AM–5:30PM EST Monday–Friday)
Generous discounts on quantity orders. SATISFACTION GUARANTEED. Prices subject to change.

Children's Books

Around the World in One Shabbat
Jewish People Celebrate the Sabbath Together
By Durga Yael Bernhard
Takes your child on a colorful adventure to share the many ways Jewish people celebrate Shabbat around the world.
11 x 8½, 32 pp, Full-color illus., HC, 978-1-58023-433-7 **$18.99** *For ages 3–6*

It's a ... It's a ... It's a Mitzvah
By Liz Suneby and Diane Heiman; Full-color Illus. by Laurel Molk
Join Mitzvah Meerkat and friends as they introduce children to the everyday kindnesses that mark the beginning of a Jewish journey and a lifetime commitment to *tikkun olam* (repairing the world). 9 x 12, 32 pp, Full-color illus., HC, 978-1-58023-509-9 **$18.99** *For ages 3–6*

What You Will See Inside a Synagogue
By Rabbi Lawrence A. Hoffman, PhD, and Dr. Ron Wolfson; Full-color photos by Bill Aron
A colorful, fun-to-read introduction that explains the ways and whys of Jewish worship and religious life. 8½ x 10½, 32 pp, Full-color photos, Quality PB, 978-1-59473-256-0 **$8.99** *For ages 6 & up*
(A book from SkyLight Paths, Jewish Lights' sister imprint)

Because Nothing Looks Like God
By Lawrence Kushner and Karen Kushner
Real-life examples of happiness and sadness—from goodnight stories, to the hope and fear felt the first time at bat, to the closing moments of someone's life—invite parents and children to explore, together, the questions we all have about God, no matter what our age. 11 x 8½, 32 pp, Full-color illus., HC, 978-1-58023-092-6 **$18.99** *For ages 4 & up*

The Book of Miracles: A Young Person's Guide to Jewish Spiritual Awareness
Written and illus. by Lawrence Kushner
Easy-to-read, imaginatively illustrated book encourages kids' awareness of their own spirituality. Revealing the essence of Judaism in a language they can understand and enjoy. 6 x 9, 96 pp, 2-color illus., HC, 978-1-879045-78-1 **$16.95** *For ages 9–13*

In God's Hands   *By Lawrence Kushner and Gary Schmidt*
Brings new life to a traditional Jewish folktale, reminding parents and kids of all faiths and all backgrounds that each of us has the power to make the world a better place—working ordinary miracles with our everyday deeds.
9 x 12, 32 pp, Full-color illus., HC, 978-1-58023-224-1 **$16.99** *For ages 5 & up*

In Our Image: God's First Creatures
By Nancy Sohn Swartz
A playful new twist to the Genesis story, God asks all of nature to offer gifts to humankind—with a promise that the humans would care for creation in return. 9 x 12, 32 pp, Full-color illus., HC, 978-1-879045-99-6 **$16.95** *For ages 4 & up*
Animated app available on Apple App Store and The Google Play Marketplace **$9.99**

The Jewish Family Fun Book, 2nd Ed.
Holiday Projects, Everyday Activities, and Travel Ideas with Jewish Themes
By Danielle Dardashti and Roni Sarig
The complete sourcebook for families wanting to put a new spin on activities for Jewish holidays, holy days and the everyday. It offers dozens of easy-to-do activities that bring Jewish tradition to life for kids of all ages.
6 x 9, 304 pp, w/ 70+ b/w illus., Quality PB, 978-1-58023-333-0 **$18.99**

What Makes Someone a Jew?   *By Lauren Seidman*
Reflects the changing face of American Judaism. Helps preschoolers and young readers (ages 3–6) understand that you don't have to look a certain way to be Jewish.
10 x 8½, 32 pp, Full-color photos, Quality PB, 978-1-58023-321-7 **$8.99** *For ages 3–6*

When a Grandparent Dies: A Kid's Own Remembering Workbook for
Dealing with Shiva and the Year Beyond   *By Nechama Liss-Levinson*
8 x 10, 48 pp, 2-color text, HC, 978-1-879045-44-6 **$15.95** *For ages 7–13*

Children's Books by Sandy Eisenberg Sasso

The *Shema* in the Mezuzah: Listening to Each Other
Introduces children ages 3 to 6 to the words of the *Shema* and the custom of putting up the mezuzah. Winner, National Jewish Book Award
9 x 12, 32 pp, Full-color illus., HC, 978-1-58023-506-8 **$18.99**

Adam & Eve's First Sunset: God's New Day
Explores fear and hope, faith and gratitude in ways that will delight kids and adults—inspiring us to bless each of God's days and nights.
9 x 12, 32 pp, Full-color illus., HC, 978-1-58023-177-0 **$17.95** *For ages 4 & up*

Also Available as a Board Book: **Adam and Eve's New Day**
5 x 5, 24 pp, Full-color illus., Board Book, 978-1-59473-205-8 **$7.99** *For ages 0–4*
(A book from SkyLight Paths, Jewish Lights' sister imprint)

But God Remembered: Stories of Women from Creation to the
Promised Land   Four different stories of women—Lilith, Serach, Bityah and
the Daughters of Z—teach us important values through their faith and actions.
9 x 12, 32 pp, Full-color illus., Quality PB, 978-1-58023-372-9 **$8.99** *For ages 8 & up*

For Heaven's Sake
Heaven is often found where you least expect it.
9 x 12, 32 pp, Full-color illus., HC, 978-1-58023-054-4 **$16.95** *For ages 4 & up*

God in Between
If you wanted to find God, where would you look? This magical, mythical tale
teaches that God can be found where we are: within all of us and the relationships
between us. 9 x 12, 32 pp, Full-color illus., HC, 978-1-879045-86-6 **$16.95** *For ages 4 & up*

God Said Amen
An inspiring story about hearing the answers to our prayers.
9 x 12, 32 pp, Full-color illus., HC, 978-1-58023-080-3 **$16.95** *For ages 4 & up*

God's Paintbrush: Special 10th Anniversary Edition
Wonderfully interactive, invites children of all faiths and backgrounds to encounter God
through moments in their own lives. Provides questions adult and child can explore
together. 11 x 8¼, 32 pp, Full-color illus., HC, 978-1-58023-195-4 **$17.95** *For ages 4 & up*

Also Available as a Board Book: **I Am God's Paintbrush**
5 x 5, 24 pp, Full-color illus., Board Book, 978-1-59473-265-2 **$7.99** *For ages 0–4*
(A book from SkyLight Paths, Jewish Lights' sister imprint)

Also Available: **God's Paintbrush Teacher's Guide**
8½ x 11, 32 pp, PB, 978-1-879045-57-6 **$8.95**

God's Paintbrush Celebration Kit
A Spiritual Activity Kit for Teachers and Students of All Faiths, All Backgrounds
9½ x 12, 40 Full-color Activity Sheets & Teacher Folder w/ complete instructions
HC, 978-1-58023-050-6 **$21.95**
8-Student Activity Sheet Pack (40 sheets/5 sessions), 978-1-58023-058-2 **$19.95**

In God's Name
Like an ancient myth in its poetic text and vibrant illustrations, this award-
winning modern fable about the search for God's name celebrates the diversity
and, at the same time, the unity of all people.
9 x 12, 32 pp, Full-color illus., HC, 978-1-879045-26-2 **$16.99** *For ages 4 & up*

Also Available as a Board Book: **What Is God's Name?**
5 x 5, 24 pp, Full-color illus., Board Book, 978-1-893361-10-2 **$7.99** *For ages 0–4*
(A book from SkyLight Paths, Jewish Lights' sister imprint)

Also Available in Spanish: **El nombre de Dios**
9 x 12, 32 pp, Full-color illus., HC, 978-1-893361-63-8 **$16.95** *For ages 4 & up*

Noah's Wife: The Story of Naamah
9 x 12, 32 pp, Full-color illus., HC, 978-1-58023-134-3 **$16.95** *For ages 4 & up*

Also Available as a Board Book: **Naamah, Noah's Wife**
5 x 5, 24 pp, Full-color illus., Board Book, 978-1-893361-56-0 **$7.95** *For ages 0–4*
(A book from SkyLight Paths, Jewish Lights' sister imprint)

Graphic Novels / Graphic History

The Adventures of Rabbi Harvey: A Graphic Novel of Jewish Wisdom and Wit in the Wild West *By Steve Sheinkin* 6 x 9, 144 pp, Full-color illus., Quality PB, 978-1-58023-310-1 **$16.99**

Rabbi Harvey Rides Again: A Graphic Novel of Jewish Folktales Let Loose in the Wild West *By Steve Sheinkin* 6 x 9, 144 pp, Full-color illus., Quality PB, 978-1-58023-347-7 **$16.99**

Rabbi Harvey vs. the Wisdom Kid: A Graphic Novel of Dueling Jewish Folktales in the Wild West *By Steve Sheinkin*
6 x 9, 144 pp, Full-color illus., Quality PB, 978-1-58023-422-1 **$16.99**

The Story of the Jews: A 4,000-Year Adventure—A Graphic History Book

By Stan Mack 6 x 9, 288 pp, Illus., Quality PB, 978-1-58023-155-8 **$16.99**

Ecology / Environment

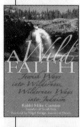

A Wild Faith: Jewish Ways into Wilderness, Wilderness Ways into Judaism *By Rabbi Mike Comins; Foreword by Nigel Savage* 6 x 9, 240 pp, Quality PB, 978-1-58023-316-3 **$16.99**

Ecology & the Jewish Spirit: Where Nature & the Sacred Meet *Edited by Ellen Bernstein* 6 x 9, 288 pp, Quality PB, 978-1-58023-082-7 **$18.99**

Torah of the Earth: Exploring 4,000 Years of Ecology in Jewish Thought Vol. 1: Biblical Israel & Rabbinic Judaism; Vol. 2: Zionism & Eco-Judaism *Edited by Rabbi Arthur Waskow* Vol. 1: 6 x 9, 272 pp, Quality PB, 978-1-58023-086-5 **$19.95** Vol. 2: 6 x 9, 336 pp, Quality PB, 978-1-58023-087-2 **$19.95**

The Way Into Judaism and the Environment *By Jeremy Benstein, PhD* 6 x 9, 288 pp, Quality PB, 978-1-58023-368-2 **$18.99**; HC, 978-1-58023-268-5 **$24.99**

Ritual / Sacred Practices

God in Your Body: Kabbalah, Mindfulness and Embodied Spiritual Practice *By Jay Michaelson* The first comprehensive treatment of the body in Jewish spiritual practice and an essential guide to the sacred. 6 x 9, 272 pp, Quality PB, 978-1-58023-304-0 **$18.99**

The Book of Jewish Sacred Practices: CLAL's Guide to Everyday & Holiday Rituals & Blessings *Edited by Rabbi Irwin Kula and Vanessa L. Ochs, PhD* 6 x 9, 368 pp, Quality PB, 978-1-58023-152-7 **$18.95**

The Jewish Dream Book: The Key to Opening the Inner Meaning of Your Dreams *By Vanessa L. Ochs, PhD, with Elizabeth Ochs; Illus. by Kristina Swarner* 8 x 8, 128 pp, Full-color illus., Deluxe PB w/ flaps, 978-1-58023-132-9 $16.95

Jewish Ritual: A Brief Introduction for Christians *By Rabbi Kerry M. Olitzky and Rabbi Daniel Judson* 5½ x 8½, 144 pp, Quality PB, 978-1-58023-210-4 **$14.99**

The Rituals & Practices of a Jewish Life: A Handbook for Personal Spiritual Renewal *Edited by Rabbi Kerry M. Olitzky and Rabbi Daniel Judson* 6 x 9, 272 pp, Illus., Quality PB, 978-1-58023-169-5 **$18.95**

The Sacred Art of Lovingkindness: Preparing to Practice *By Rabbi Rami Shapiro* 5½ x 8½, 176 pp, Quality PB, 978-1-59473-151-8 **$16.99** (A book from SkyLight Paths, Jewish Lights' sister imprint)

Mystery & Detective Fiction

Criminal Kabbalah: An Intriguing Anthology of Jewish Mystery & Detective Fiction *Edited by Lawrence W. Raphael; Foreword by Laurie R. King* All-new stories from twelve of today's masters of mystery and detective fiction— sure to delight mystery buffs of all faith traditions. 6 x 9, 256 pp, Quality PB, 978-1-58023-109-1 **$16.95**

Mystery Midrash: An Anthology of Jewish Mystery & Detective Fiction *Edited by Lawrence W. Raphael; Preface by Joel Siegel* 6 x 9, 304 pp, Quality PB, 978-1-58023-055-1 **$16.95**

Bar / Bat Mitzvah

The Mitzvah Project Book
Making Mitzvah Part of Your Bar/Bat Mitzvah ... and Your Life
By Liz Suneby and Diane Heiman; Foreword by Rabbi Jeffrey K. Salkin; Preface by Rabbi Sharon Brous
The go-to source for Jewish young adults and their families looking to make the
world a better place through good deeds—big or small.
6 x 9, 224 pp, Quality PB Original, 978-1-58023-458-0 **$16.99** *For ages 11–13*

The Bar/Bat Mitzvah Memory Book, 2nd Edition: An Album for Treasuring
the Spiritual Celebration
By Rabbi Jeffrey K. Salkin and Nina Salkin
8 x 10, 48 pp, 2-color text, Deluxe HC, ribbon marker, 978-1-58023-263-0 **$19.99**

For Kids—Putting God on Your Guest List, 2nd Edition: How to Claim the
Spiritual Meaning of Your Bar or Bat Mitzvah *By Rabbi Jeffrey K. Salkin*
6 x 9, 144 pp, Quality PB, 978-1-58023-308-8 **$15.99** *For ages 11–13*

The Jewish Prophet: Visionary Words from Moses and Miriam to Henrietta Szold
and A. J. Heschel *By Rabbi Dr. Michael J. Shire*
6½ x 8½, 128 pp, 123 full-color illus., HC, 978-1-58023-168-8 **$14.95**

Putting God on the Guest List, 3rd Edition: How to Reclaim the Spiritual
Meaning of Your Child's Bar or Bat Mitzvah *By Rabbi Jeffrey K. Salkin*
6 x 9, 224 pp, Quality PB, 978-1-58023-222-7 **$16.99**
        Teacher's Guide: 8½ x 11, 48 pp, PB, 978-1-58023-226-5 **$8.99**

Teens / Young Adults

Text Messages: A Torah Commentary for Teens
Edited by Rabbi Jeffrey K. Salkin
Shows today's teens how each Torah portion contains worlds of meaning for
them, for what they are going through in their lives, and how they can shape their
Jewish identity as they enter adulthood.
6 x 9, 304 pp (est), HC, 978-1-58023-507-5 **$24.99**

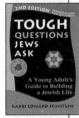

Hannah Senesh: Her Life and Diary, the First Complete Edition
By Hannah Senesh; Foreword by Marge Piercy; Preface by Eitan Senesh; Afterword by Roberta Grossman
6 x 9, 368 pp, b/w photos, Quality PB, 978-1-58023-342-2 **$19.99**

I Am Jewish: Personal Reflections Inspired by the Last Words of Daniel Pearl
Edited by Judea and Ruth Pearl 6 x 9, 304 pp, Deluxe PB w/ flaps, 978-1-58023-259-3 **$19.99**
Download a free copy of the *I Am Jewish Teacher's Guide* at www.jewishlights.com.

The JGirl's Guide: The Young Jewish Woman's Handbook for Coming of Age
By Penina Adelman, Ali Feldman and Shulamit Reinharz
6 x 9, 240 pp, Quality PB, 978-1-58023-215-9 **$14.99** *For ages 11 & up*
        Teacher's & Parent's Guide: 8½ x 11, 56 pp, PB, 978-1-58023-225-8 **$8.99**

The JGuy's Guide: The GPS for Jewish Teen Guys
By Rabbi Joseph B. Meszler, Dr. Shulamit Reinharz, Liz Suneby and Diane Heiman
6 x 9, 208 pp, Quality PB Original, 978-1-58023-721-5 **$16.99**
        Teacher's Guide: 8½ x 11, 30pp, PB, 978-1-58023-773-4 **$8.99**

Tough Questions Jews Ask, 2nd Edition: A Young Adult's Guide to Building a
Jewish Life *By Rabbi Edward Feinstein*
6 x 9, 160 pp, Quality PB, 978-1-58023-454-2 **$16.99** *For ages 11 & up*
        Teacher's Guide: 8½ x 11, 72 pp, PB, 978-1-58023-187-9 **$8.95**

Pre-Teens

Be Like God: God's To-Do List for Kids
By Dr. Ron Wolfson
Encourages kids ages eight through twelve to use their God-given superpowers
to find the many ways they can make a difference in the lives of others and find
meaning and purpose for their own.
7 x 9, 144 pp, Quality PB, 978-1-58023-510-5 **$15.99** *For ages 8–12*

The Book of Miracles: A Young Person's Guide to Jewish Spiritual Awareness
By Lawrence Kushner, with all-new illustrations by the author.
6 x 9, 96 pp, 2-color illus., HC, 978-1-879045-78-1 **$16.95** *For ages 9–13*

About Jewish Lights

People of all faiths and backgrounds yearn for books that attract, engage, educate, and spiritually inspire.

Our principal goal is to stimulate thought and help all people learn about who the Jewish People are, where they come from, and what the future can be made to hold. While people of our diverse Jewish heritage are the primary audience, our books speak to people in the Christian world as well and will broaden their understanding of Judaism and the roots of their own faith.

We bring to you authors who are at the forefront of spiritual thought and experience. While each has something different to say, they all say it in a voice that you can hear.

Our books are designed to welcome you and then to engage, stimulate, and inspire. We judge our success not only by whether or not our books are beautiful and commercially successful, but by whether or not they make a difference in your life.

For your information and convenience, at the back of this book we have provided a list of other Jewish Lights books you might find interesting and useful. They cover all the categories of your life:

Bar/Bat Mitzvah	Life Cycle
Bible Study / Midrash	Meditation
Children's Books	Men's Interest
Congregation Resources	Parenting
Current Events / History	Prayer / Ritual / Sacred Practice
Ecology / Environment	Social Justice
Fiction: Mystery, Science Fiction	Spirituality
Grief / Healing	Theology / Philosophy
Holidays / Holy Days	Travel
Inspiration	Twelve Steps
Kabbalah / Mysticism / Enneagram	Women's Interest

Stuart M. Matlins, Publisher

Or phone, fax, mail or e-mail to: **JEWISH LIGHTS Publishing**
Sunset Farm Offices, Route 4 • P.O. Box 237 • Woodstock, Vermont 05091
Tel: (802) 457-4000 • Fax: (802) 457-4004 • www.jewishlights.com
Credit card orders: **(800) 962-4544** (8:30AM–5:30PM EST Monday–Friday)
Generous discounts on quantity orders. SATISFACTION GUARANTEED. Prices subject to change.

For more information about each book, visit our website at www.jewishlights.com